What others ar

"If you own a business, you need to talk with Tony. He educates you on the complex tax laws and business principles you need to run your business more efficiently and effectively."

–Mike Musaelian, Small Business Consultant

"Being a former IRS Auditor gives Tony a huge advantage in knowing the system from both sides. I consider myself lucky to have found him and advise all of my friends, colleagues, and you, to talk with Tony."

–Joe Gleason, CEO of Primo Strategies, LLC

"Tony makes my previous CPAs look like amateurs. He has a unique perspective as a former IRS Auditor, which helps business owners minimize their tax burden in a justifiable manner. He genuinely wants to do the best possible for his clients."

–Brian Chou, Partner of EyeLux Optometry

"As a new business owner, I had a mountain of questions, problems, and tax stress that seemed impossible to overcome. Tony took the time to go over everything that I would need to do to stay on track and be successful in my business."

–Lora Haliw, CEO of Spaw Day Mobile Grooming, LLC

"Going to Tony feels like watching NFL after watching peewee your whole life—this guy is a pro. Even the areas that he tells you he's not an expert in, he's an expert in. I cannot overstate the sense of relief I have knowing that as I grow my business I've got the most knowledgeable CPA imaginable on my team to consult with through every phase of our growth."

–Brian Graddon, Owner of CPR1

"Tony is so knowledgeable and offers great advice for taxes, business, and so much more! He knows the ins and outs of tax law and is full of helpful information."

–Tiffany Rohrer, Partner of Toot Sweet 4 Two, LLC

"Tony is an absolute standout in an otherwise difficult to navigate industry. Tony has spent hours getting me up to speed with my small business."

–Peter Bluvas, President of Peter J. Bluvas Medical Corporation

"Tony's focus on educating clients about the tax law adds a layer of value to tax service I have not experienced in the 20+ years I've been filing taxes. He has done a fabulous job helping us identify ways to maximize our deductions and minimize our fear of doing it wrong. Every time we meet with him we become more confident about our financial future."

–Debra Baker, CEO of Legal Vertical Strategies, LLC

"When it comes to taxes, my head starts spinning. Tony puts me at ease. He breaks everything down for me and makes sense of what needs to be done. He helped me setup my business correctly."

–Brittany Mason, Owner of Mazun General

"As someone who hates dealing with taxes to the point of kicking and screaming like a little child, Tony has made tax planning a very positive and knowledgeable experience for me. I'm relieved I found Tony."

–George Makris, Owner of Lucid Mastering

"After meeting with Tony, he has become my go-to guy for taxes. This guy really knows tax law. I thought I had tough tax questions, but Tony answered them with ease and gave me useful tax strategies. I now always turn to Tony when I have tax questions and I recommend you do too!"

–Ian Guinn, Consultant

"Tony is wonderful! He has more knowledge about taxes and tax law than I have ever come across. Thank you so much for all of your hard work!"

–**Carmen Ridenoure, Owner of Reaction Photography**

"Tony is awesome! I learned more from him in our meetings than I have from any other accountant/tax preparer that I've used in the past. He's honest, genuine, and thorough."

–**Tita Gray, Consultant**

"Tony is about as competent as they come in his industry. His years of experience, backed with his stellar educational history makes him the tax guy. There wasn't a question he couldn't answer and you could see his passion to figure out a solution to my particular situation."

–**David Martiarena, Owner of San Diego Paella**

"Tony is a tax god! He really helped us out on our messed up multi-state filing this year. With his experience with the government, I'm sure he's getting us all of our deductions and a great refund. Thanks Tony, you're the best!"

–**Jimmy Greene, Photographer**

"I'm so glad I found Tony. He provided me with information, advice, and a tax plan so I can better prepare for the next year. I was very impressed with Tony's knowledge and willingness to share so much information about the tax laws and business strategies."

–**Nancy Boyd, President of Financial Essentials, Inc.**

"Tony walked me though everything step-by-step and helped me maximize my deductions for my small business. He knows all the ins and outs and is straight up about everything. I highly recommend him to everyone."

–**Chuck Lehneis, ESL Teacher**

OUTSMARTING THE SYSTEM

LOWER YOUR TAXES, CONTROL YOUR FUTURE, AND REACH FINANCIAL FREEDOM

Anthony C. Campidonica, CPA, EA, MBA, MSA
Former IRS Agent

Sciopress, Inc.
7770 Regents Road, Suite # 113-227
San Diego, CA 92122

Cover and illustrations: Courtesy of Becky Cohen

Library of Congress Control Number: 2013957614

ISBN 978-0-9913029-7-0

*This book is dedicated to those who strive to obtain
financial freedom and continually search for strategies
to get there faster. It is intended to be a tool to
use on your journey.*

Visit www.OutsmartingTheSystem.com for updates.

CONTENTS

About the Author

Anthony C. Campidonica (Tony) has been providing small business consulting since 1998 and tax services since 2001. He is a Certified Public Accountant (CPA) in California and an Enrolled Agent (EA). He holds a Master of Business Administration (MBA) and a Master of Science in Accountancy (MSA).

Tony spent over eight years as an Internal Revenue Agent (tax auditor) with the Internal Revenue Service (IRS). This experience provided Tony with unique insight of tax laws and the opportunities provided to the rich. Tony excelled at the IRS, was promoted quickly, and earned numerous awards.

Most recently, he started his own consulting company, StrataTax®, aimed at helping individuals and small businesses reach their financial and strategic goals. Tony shows people how to secure their future as he coaches them on the formation, growth, and taxation of their businesses. He has consistently turned employees into successful business owners.

Tony has been praised by his clients and colleagues for his ability to simplify complex terms and strategies. Using his guidance, many of his clients are now taking advantage of the tax opportunities made available to the rich. Their reduced tax liabilities and enhanced business knowledge have put them on the path to financial freedom.

Tony was prompted to write this book for two reasons. First, he believes that everyone—not just the rich—need to be aware of the constraints of the system and the opportunities provided to them through the tax laws. Second, he wrote this book because so many of his clients encouraged him to help others as he helped them. Now Tony is revealing to you the strategies for outsmarting the system.

- CHAPTER 1 -

Purpose

✧ Do you feel broke no matter how much money you make?

✧ Are you worried you'll never get ahead?

✧ Do you think you're paying too much in taxes?

✧ Do you believe the rich don't pay their fair share of taxes?

✧ Did you buy into a system that has let you down?

If you answered yes to any of these questions, this book is for you.

Taxes are your largest expense. They significantly reduce your income and can lead to feelings of helplessness and frustration. Paying too much in taxes can prevent you from reaching financial freedom.

What is financial freedom?

Financial freedom is having enough money saved to support your lifestyle without needing to work.

The rich aren't faced with the same problems as the average taxpayer. They're outsmarting the system and reducing their taxes. This book explains how to take advantage of the tax laws in the same way as the rich.

The U.S. tax laws are the most complex in the world. Albert Einstein said it best, "The hardest thing in the world to understand is the income tax." And the tax laws have only gotten more complex since he made that statement! If it was confusing to that famed genius of the modern era, how is an average taxpayer supposed to understand it?

Throughout this book, I'll decrypt these complex laws for you. Unless otherwise noted, the tax laws mentioned in this book are based on the federal tax laws as of December 2013. All of the strategies mentioned in this book are legal and are in no way intended to defraud the U.S. government. The often quoted Federal Judge Learned Hand explained in *Helvering v. Gregory*, 69 F.2d 809, 810-11 (2d Cir. 1934), "Any one may so arrange his affairs that his taxes shall be as low as possible; he is not bound to choose that pattern which will best pay the Treasury; there is not even a patriotic duty to increase one's taxes." This is exactly what the rich do, so why don't you?!

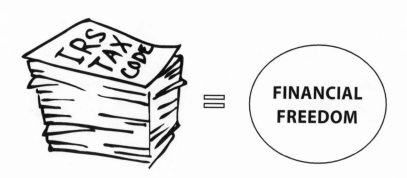

There is a difference between tax evasion and tax avoidance. Tax evasion is the intent to defraud the U.S. government by reducing one's tax liability through illegal means. For instance, if you intentionally didn't report $1,000,000 of income on your tax return, the Internal Revenue Service (IRS) would most likely pursue fraud charges against you. Tax avoidance is the structuring of one's financial affairs in a legal manner to reduce or optimize one's tax liability. You're allowed to implement tax avoidance strategies and I'll show you how.

To be clear, I do believe in paying taxes. I agree with Supreme Court Justice Oliver Wendell Holmes, Jr. who said, "Taxes are the price we pay for a civilized society." Taxes pay for our national defense, health care, public schools, roads, social services, fire protection, law enforcement, water and land management, and many other services. I don't advocate not paying taxes, however, I do encourage all of you to structure your financial affairs in a way that minimizes your taxes and enables you to reach financial freedom.

The strategies in this book are based on my experiences with the rich. I've spent a significant amount of time learning how people in America became wealthy on their own. In addition, I've experienced first-hand how average people have lowered their taxes, controlled their future, and reached financial freedom by implementing the strategies discussed in this book.

This book is written for the busy individual who has limited time to read, such as an employee, parent, investor, landlord, or business owner. It's written as short and succinct as possible so it can be read in a minimal amount of time. I encourage you to re-read this book as many times as necessary until you completely understand how to decrease your taxes by changing the way you make your money.

This book is written from a high-level perspective to illustrate overall strategies. It's intended to open up your mind to different ways of making money and lowering your taxes. I strongly encourage you to seek additional guidance from professional advisors prior to implementing any of these strategies. Chapter 8 includes information on how to choose a trusted advisor.

Lastly, having access to the Internet while you read this book will help you better understand the concepts. Since this book is written at a high-level, I don't define every technical word and I don't include copies of the tax forms. Including this information could distract you from the main concepts and strategies taught throughout the book. Definitions are available on the Internet. Tax forms are available on the IRS's website at www.irs.gov. Remember to focus on the main points in this book and talk to professionals to learn the details.

CHAPTER 2

Problem

Most Americans strive for the same thing: financial freedom. Financial freedom is the day you don't have to work anymore because you have enough money saved to support your lifestyle for the rest of your life. Some people call this retirement; they save money each year in hopes that they'll have enough money to live on until they die. For the purposes of this book, financial freedom is synonymous with retirement.

The biggest obstacle to achieving financial freedom is the system people have been programmed to follow. As children, people are taught to get good grades in high school, attend college, get good grades in college, graduate, find a job as an employee, get a promotion, buy a house to live in, and put money into a retirement account. People are led to believe that following this system will ensure financial freedom. However, it often makes financial freedom unattainable for most Americans. This system is flawed and taxes are the culprit!

> The system is the path that most people pursue. You should subvert the dominant paradigm, or challenge the main way of thinking, to make sure it's the right path for you.

The System

College

The system encourages people to become employees. America was founded by entrepreneurs, including your ancestors, who took a risk to leave their countries in search of a better life in America. However, since the early 1900s, the focus has switched from becoming an entrepreneur to becoming an employee.

The National Center for Education Statistics (NCES) is the federal organization that collects and analyzes data related to education. According to the NCES, college attendance has increased each fall term since the early 1900s. College enrollment was 21.0 million students in fall 2010, higher than in any previous year, and it's expected to continue setting new records from fall 2011 through fall 2020. This is a major problem for America because colleges primarily produce employees.

Colleges prepare people to graduate with a degree in hopes that an organization will hire them. People spend most of their life preparing to work and don't learn how to make money on their own. The challenge in recent years is that these organizations haven't been hiring. Consequently, many college graduates are unemployed and at a loss. To make matters worse, most college students have loans to repay. Not working and not earning money makes it hard to pay off debt!

Employee

Even if you are one of the lucky ones to have a job, the system has programmed you to work hard at your job to earn more money. This is foolish! When you're an employee and work, who gets paid first by your employer? Unfortunately, it's not you!

The IRS and the state taxing agency, depending on where you work, are the first to get paid. It's a federal law for your employer to withhold taxes for the IRS before you receive the money you earned. Is this fair? It's the government that benefits when people buy into the system and become employees.

Contrary to what most people think, the solution to this problem isn't to make more money at your job. Let's say that you're an employee, you're good at what you do, and you receive a promotion and pay increase. Your taxes will increase because as you make more money, the government taxes you more. How's that for rewarding you?

Home Purchase

Next, the system has you programmed to buy a house to live in as your primary residence because you can write off your mortgage insurance premiums, points, home mortgage interest, and real estate taxes on your tax return, which will decrease your taxes. This is the smart move, right?

Unfortunately, you may not be able to write off all of those expenses related to your primary residence. If you make too much money, you can't deduct the mortgage insurance premiums. Deducting points is a one-time deduction, unless you refinance, in which case some of the points are deductible each year. Now you're down to writing off only two expenses: (1) the home mortgage interest, and (2) real estate taxes. Both of these are considered itemized deductions on your personal tax return and get phased out if you make too much money. Note that I didn't mention repairs, improvements, homeowners insurance, homeowners association (HOA) fees, appliances, or furniture above. Those are considered personal expenses and therefore, you can't deduct them.

Retirement Account

The system emphasizes that the next step on the path to financial freedom is to put money into a retirement account. Another smart move, right? When you have extra money to invest, your primary options are to put the money in a personal brokerage account or contribute towards a retirement account, such as a Traditional 401(k) at your job. Most tax professionals advise that it's more advantageous to invest through a personal account if you expect to be in the same or a higher tax bracket when you withdraw the money. Conversely, most tax professionals advise that it's more advantageous to invest through a retirement account if you expect to be in a lower tax bracket. This is due to the timing of when your money will be taxed. Identifying which tax bracket you'll be in when you retire will help you decide which investment account is most advantageous for you. Let's walk through a simplified scenario that illustrates your different options and the tax implications and timing of each.

Scenario

✧ You're currently in the 25% marginal tax bracket for federal income tax purposes (your ordinary income tax rate)

✧ You purchased one share of stock for $100

✧ You sold that share of stock after one year for $120

Your long-term capital gain is $20. A long-term capital gain is when you sell an asset that you've owned for over a year at a gain.

$120 price now - $100 purchase price = $20 capital gain

Options

Option One – Personal Brokerage Account

For stock purchased through your personal brokerage account, long-term capital gains are taxed at 15%. In this option, your $20 gain is taxed at 15%, or $3.

$20 gain x 15% tax rate = $3 tax

Option Two – Traditional 401(k) Account

You purchase the same share of stock through a retirement account, such as a Traditional 401(k) account, at your job because that's what the system has taught you to do. The money you contribute is pre-tax now, but will be taxed when you take it out of the account in the future. In this example, the gain will be taxed at your ordinary income tax rate of 25%, or $5.

$20 gain x 25% tax rate = $5 tax

Comparison

In this scenario, taxes are $2 lower when an investment is made through a personal brokerage account rather than a Traditional 401(k) account. $2 is small, but if you start to multiply this by a $1,000, $10,000, or $100,000, the difference becomes more material. Did you know all of this?

	Personal Brokerage	**Traditional 401(k)**
Tax Rate	15%	25%
Stock sold after 1 year	$120	$120
- Stock Purchase Price	$100	$100
= Gain	$20	$20
Tax Now	$3	$0
Tax Later	$0	$5
Total Tax	$3	$5
Difference	*$2 less in taxes through the personal brokerage account*	

As shown above, if you purchase a stock, mutual fund, exchange traded fund (ETF), or any other asset in your 401(k) account and held that asset for over a year before you sold it at a gain, you'll miss out on the preferential long-term capital gains tax rate.

Another potential disadvantage of contributing to your 401(k) account is the risk of penalties for early distributions. If you take a distribution from your 401(k) account before you reach age 59 ½ and you don't meet an exception to this penalty, you're subject to an additional tax penalty of 10% from the IRS and possible state penalties (in California it's 2.5%). How unfair is that? It's your money! The system misled you again!

Overview

You don't need a college degree to reach your financial freedom. There have been plenty of successful people in America who haven't graduated from college, such as Bill Gates, Steve Jobs, Michael Dell, and Mark Zuckerberg. What you need, to reach your financial freedom, is a better understanding that the financial path you've been taught to follow may not actually be the best path for you.

The system is unfair, but there is a solution. With the knowledge from this book, a plan, and action, you can make a change to start decreasing your taxes. This change will enable you to save more money and reach financial freedom faster. You can't control what happens around you, but you can control what you do. Success will not happen overnight for you. It'll take time.

The following chapters will provide you with the knowledge you need to start reaching financial freedom faster.

- CHAPTER 3 -

Process

To understand the solution, it's essential to first understand the process through which income is reported to the IRS and how a tax liability is calculated.

Tax System

The U.S. Congress, not the IRS, creates the tax laws in America. Most tax legislation begins in the House of Representatives where these laws are considered by the Ways and Means Committee. Upon approval by the House of Representatives, the bill is sent to the Senate where it's considered by the Senate Finance Committee. After approval of the bill, it's forwarded to the President for signing. If the President signs the bill, the new legislation is incorporated into the Internal Revenue Code (IRC), which is also known as Title 26 of the United States Code (USC).

Tax System

Tax Law - Internal Revenue Code or Title 26 of the United States Code
President Signs ⇧
Senate - Senate Finance Committee ⇧
House of Representatives - Ways and Means Committee ⇧

Who influences Congress to write these laws? People and organizations with money. When the wealthy influence Congress, what are they trying to do with the tax laws? Lower it for themselves through special tax relief provisions. If these tax relief provisions are written for the rich, then the trick is for you to receive your money in the same way as the rich.

Federal Income Tax Return – Form 1040

Let's review what a tax return looks like to get a better understanding of how our federal tax laws work. Go ahead and pull out your most recent federal individual income tax return, Form 1040, or download a copy of the most recent version of the "Form 1040" from the Internet. The Form 1040 has two pages.

You may have filed a Form 1040A or Form 1040EZ, but use a Form 1040 to review. All of these forms follow the same basic principles. The main difference is that a Form 1040EZ is the most basic form. It doesn't have as much information being reported on it. The Form 1040, also known as the long form, allows for everything to be reported on it. The Form 1040A is in the middle of the Form 1040EZ and Form 1040 in regards to the number of items you can report on it.

Personal Information, Filing Status, Exemptions

At the top of page 1 of the Form 1040 is a section for all of your personal information. Report your filing status and exemptions below your personal information. Your filing status and exemptions are important because they're used in calculating your taxable income. Filing status includes single, married filing jointly, married filing separately, head of household, or qualifying widow(er) with a dependent child. Exemptions include you, a spouse, and any dependents.

Income

In the following section, report your income, such as wages, taxable interest, dividends, long-term capital gains, business income, and unemployment compensation.

Adjustments

Below the income section, make adjustments to your income, such as educator expenses, a Traditional IRA deduction, or student loan interest deduction. These adjustments are known as deductions. A tax deduction reduces your taxable income. Deductions are different than tax credits, which are discussed in a following section.

Adjusted Gross Income

Subtracting these adjustments from your income will result in an amount called adjusted gross income (AGI). This number is the most important number on your tax return because it directly impacts the amount of taxes you'll pay. The higher your AGI, the more taxes you'll pay.

Your AGI also impacts the amount of some tax deductions. For instance, for 2013, if you had over $155,000 of income and filed jointly, or over $75,000 of income and filed single, you couldn't deduct any of your student loan interest payments made in 2013.

Likewise, your AGI also impacts the amount of some tax credits. If you had over $180,000 of income and filed jointly, or over $90,000 of income and filed single, you couldn't claim the American Opportunity Credit, which is an education credit.

Standard/Itemized Deductions and Exemptions

Go to the top of page 2 of the Form 1040. From your AGI, you get to subtract the higher of a standard deduction or the total of your itemized deductions. You cannot deduct both of these; you can only deduct one. In most cases, it's more beneficial to deduct the higher one because it lowers your AGI more. The lower your AGI, the less taxes you'll pay.

The amount of your standard deduction is based on your filing status. It's determined by the tax laws each year and is printed on the Form 1040.

2013 Standard Deductions

Filing Status	Standard Deduction
Single or Married Filing Separately	$6,100
Married Filing Jointly or Qualifying Widow(er)	$12,200
Head of Household	$8,950

The most common itemized deductions include state income taxes, mortgage interest, real estate property taxes, and charitable donations. Gifts to charity can be made in cash or non cash, such as clothes, electronics, and furniture. Most taxpayers take the standard deduction rather than itemized deductions on their tax return because the amount of their standard deduction is higher than the total of their itemized deductions.

If your AGI is too high ($300,000 if filing jointly or $250,000 if filing single) your itemized deductions will start to phase out and you won't be able to claim the full deduction. This is another way the government taxes you more if you make more money.

You also get to subtract your exemptions from your AGI. You get one exemption for each person filing the return and one for each dependent claimed on the return. Tax laws determine the exemption amount each year. It's printed on the Form 1040. For 2013, the exemption amount is $3,900 per person.

Similar to the itemized deduction phase out, the personal exemption will start to phase out if your AGI is too high ($300,000 if filing jointly or $250,000 if filing single) and you won't get the full exemption.

Taxable Income and Tax

Your AGI minus the standard deduction or itemized deductions, minus exemptions, results in taxable income. Taxable income is then put into a complex table to calculate your tax. You can review Publication 17 on the IRS's website at www.irs.gov for a more detailed explanation of how to calculate your tax.

2013 Federal Individual Ordinary Income Tax Brackets (Based on Taxable Income)

Tax Rate	Single Filers	Married Filing Jointly or Qualifying Widow(er)	Married Filing Separately	Head of Household
10%	$0 - $8,925	$0 - $17,850	$0 - $8,925	$0 - $12,750
15%	$8,926 - $36,250	$17,851 - $72,500	$8,926 - $36,250	$12,751 - $48,600
25%	$36,251 - $87,850	$72,501 - $146,400	$36,251 - $73,200	$48,601 - $125,450
28%	$87,851 - $183,250	$146,401 - $223,050	$73,201 - $111,525	$125,451 - $203,150
33%	$183,251 - $398,350	$223,051 - $398,350	$111,526 - $199,175	$203,151 - $398,350
35%	$398,351 - $400,000	$398,351 - $450,000	$199,176 - $225,000	$398,351 - $425,000
39.6%	$400,001 or more	$450,001 or more	$225,001 or more	$425,001 or more

Credits

After calculating your tax, you get to subtract out any credits, such as the child and dependent care expense credit or the child tax credit.

A credit directly reduces your tax liability. Some credits are refundable, meaning they're not limited to just your tax liability. With a refundable credit, you could still get a refund even though you don't owe any tax. Therefore, a credit is typically more beneficial than a deduction. For example, if your total tax liability was only $500 and you had a re-fundable credit for $700, such as the American Opportunity Credit for a dependent attending undergraduate college, you would get a refund of $200.

Again, if your AGI is above a certain threshold, you could lose a credit. These thresholds are determined by the tax laws each year.

Total Tax

The end result is total tax. Combine the amount of federal income tax you had withheld from your job with the total of estimated tax payments, if any. The difference between the total tax and your withholdings and/or payments will result in either a refund or an amount that you owe.

The Form 1040 can be simplified as:

All Income – Adjustments to Income = Adjusted Gross Income (AGI)

AGI – Deductions – Exemptions = Taxable Income

Taxable Income x Tax Rate = Tax

Tax – Credits = Total Tax

Goal

Your goal is to have your AGI, and resulting taxable income, as low as possible each year. A low AGI will decrease your taxable income and therefore decrease your tax liability.

Refunds

The system uses our cryptic tax laws to fool everyone into believing big refunds on your tax return are good. Big refunds are not good! A big refund means you let the government use your money interest-free throughout the year. You could've used that money to invest, earning at least interest from a savings account.

In addition, the government could delay paying you a refund if there's a budget crisis or government shutdown. For example, due to budget constraints in 2009, the California Franchise Tax Board was unable to pay its residents awaiting income tax refunds and had to issue them IOU ("I owe you") letters. Due to the 16-day government shutdown in October 2013, the IRS delayed issuing refunds owed to taxpayers at that time. For these reasons, it's best to not have a big refund.

U.S. Tax Laws Simplified

The U.S. tax laws are the most complex in the world, but they can be oversimplified as such: "all income is taxable, except for…". The "except for" consists of a list of non-taxable income, deductions, and credits.

U.S. Tax Laws Simplified

All Income is Taxable

- Except for...

- ✧ Tax-Exempt Interest
- ✧ Educator Expenses
- ✧ Traditional IRA Deduction
- ✧ Student Loan Interest Deduction
- ✧ Standard Deduction or Itemized Deductions, such as:

  - State Income Taxes
  - Mortgage Interest Paid
  - Real Estate Property Taxes
  - Charitable Donations

- ✧ Etcetera
- ✧ *Credits*

= Total Tax

Now that you're armed with a better understanding of how income tax liabilities are calculated, let's identify solutions that will help you outsmart the system and lower your taxes.

- CHAPTER 4 -

Solution

I've always been fascinated by how people in America became wealthy on their own. I talked to as many successful
people as I could to learn how they did it. Most of them I
met on a consulting engagement, preparing their tax return,
or while auditing them at the IRS. I also read as much as I
could about successful people to learn how they made their
fortune. I read books about Bill Gates, Warren Buffett, Sam
Walton, Henry Ford, John D. Rockefeller, Andrew Carnegie
and many others. After years of research, I discovered there
are achievable ways to become wealthy on your own and
obtain financial freedom quickly.

Excluding celebrities and professional athletes, the rich
implement particular strategies to reach financial freedom.
Through these strategies, they lower their taxes by changing
the way they make money. They can be broken down into
three groups of people: (1) investor, (2) landlord, and (3)
small business owner.

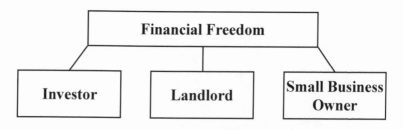

Note that none of these groups include being an employee. When you're an employee, you go to work and the government takes part of your money for taxes, such as the federal income tax, Social Security tax, Medicare tax, state income tax, and any other local and/or state tax, before you get paid. Then after you're paid, you're subject to more taxes such as the sales tax, use tax, and property taxes. For many Americans, their total taxes are close to or above 50% of their income. Investors, landlords, and small business owners minimize their taxes as much as possible by taking advantage of the tax laws.

Let's look at each group so you can learn where you need to focus your energy to decrease your taxes and reach financial freedom faster.

Investor

Some of the richest people in America, including Warren Buffett, Peter Lynch, and George Soros, are investors. They use their money in order to gain a financial return. For instance, it's common for investors to purchase stock in a corporation in hopes that the stock price will increase so they can make money when they sell it. To clarify, in the following discussion we are referring to investments made in personal accounts, not in traditional retirement accounts, such as a 401(k).

There are many different types of investments, including, but not limited to, gold, silver, stock in a corporation, bonds, certificate of deposit (CD), mutual fund, exchange traded fund (ETF), money market account, and savings account. A search on the Internet can provide you with detailed descriptions for each of these terms.

The goal of investing is to have your money work for you, i.e., increase in value, without you being there like your job requires. With investing, an investment can increase in value and earn more money for the investor without the investor being there. Conversely, an employee has to work each hour to earn money. Employees work for money, while investors make money work for them.

Being an investor can help you reach your financial freedom faster because of the preferential tax treatments for tax-exempt interest, qualified dividends, and long-term capital gains.

Tax-Exempt Interest

Tax-exempt interest income is commonly earned by investing in state or municipal bonds. A bond is a debt obligation issued by the government to fund operations. The interest on a bond used to finance these operations is typically not taxable. The higher your tax rate, the more savings you'll realize from earning tax-exempt interest income versus taxable income.

Qualified Dividends

A dividend is received when an investor owns stock in a corporation and the corporation distributes part of its profits to investors. Not all dividends are qualified dividends. Generally, to be a qualified dividend, it must be paid by a U.S. corporation or qualified foreign corporation and you must meet the holding period requirement. You can review Publication 17 on the IRS's website at www.irs.gov for a more detailed explanation of qualified dividends.

Dividends that are not qualified are taxed at your ordinary income tax rate. Qualified dividends are taxed at 0%, 15% or 20% depending on your ordinary income tax bracket. Visit page 20 to see what tax bracket you're in and compare it to the chart below.

2013 Tax Rates for Qualified Dividends

Type of Income	Holding Period	Top Rate for Taxpayers in 10% or 15% Tax Brackets	Top Rate for Taxpayers in 25%, 28%, 33%, or 35% Tax Brackets	Top Rate for Taxpayers in 39.6% Tax Bracket
Qualified dividends	N/A	0%	15%	20%

For instance, if you're in the 25% tax bracket and you receive $1,000 of qualified dividends, you would only pay $150 of federal income tax (15% tax) rather than $250 (25% tax). That's a $100 savings. As the amount of qualified dividends you receive increases, the savings increase.

Long-Term Capital Gains

The tax laws do not define what a capital asset is. It only defines what a capital asset is not.

Below is a list of what is not a capital asset:

✧ Inventory used in a business

✧ Depreciable business property used in a business

✧ Copyright, a literary, music, or artistic composition, or similar property held by a taxpayer

✧ Accounts or notes receivable acquired in the ordinary course of business for services or sale of inventory

✧ U.S. Government publication

You can read Internal Revenue Code (IRC) Section 1221 for a more detailed explanation of capital assets.

Examples of a capital asset are:

✧ Stocks held for investment

✧ Bonds held for investment

✧ Works of art held for investment

✧ Personal residence

✧ Household furnishings

✧ Personal automobile

✧ Personal boat

✧ Personal jewelry

If you sell a capital asset that you owned for over a year, the gain would be taxed at 0%, 15% or 20% depending on which ordinary income tax bracket you're in. If you sell a capital asset that you owned for a year or less, the gain would be taxed at your ordinary income tax rate.

2013 Tax Rates for Capital Gains

Type of Income	Holding Period	Top Rate for Taxpayers in 10% or 15% Tax Brackets	Top Rate for Taxpayers in 25%, 28%, 33%, or 35% Tax Brackets	Top Rate for Taxpayers in 39.6% Tax Bracket
Short-term capital gain	Up to 1 year	Ordinary income tax rate	Ordinary income tax rate	Ordinary income tax rate
Long-term capital gain	Over 1 year	0%	15%	20%

Being an investor can help lower your taxes substantially through tax-exempt interest income, qualified dividends, and/or long-term capital gains. To see a good example of this, you can do a search on the Internet for Mitt Romney's 2010 tax return. To be clear, this is not a Democrat or Republican issue. Taxes are imposed equally on members of both parties and members of both parties take advantage of these low tax rates. I use Mitt's tax return as an example because it's one of the few tax returns that is public and illustrates how someone receives preferential tax treatment for being an investor.

On Mitt's 2010 tax return, you can see that he had an effective tax rate of 13.9%, which is calculated by taking line 60, Total Tax, of $3,009,766 and dividing it by line 22, Total Income, of $21,661,344. What was your effective tax rate? Was it higher?

$$\frac{\$3,009,766 \text{ total tax}}{\$21,661,344 \text{ total income}} = 13.9\% \text{ effective tax rate}$$

His earnings include the following:

- ✧ Wages: $0

- ✧ Tax-Exempt Interest Income: $557

- ✧ Qualified Dividends: $3,327,678

- ✧ Capital Gains: $12,573,249, of which $12,118,710 were taxed as long-term capital gains

Did you notice how much he earned in wages? He was paid $0 in wages. That's right, zero dollars!

Almost all of Mitt's income for 2010 received preferential tax treatment. Where did almost all of your money come from? Was it wages? If so, you need to change the way you make money!

After reviewing Mitt's tax return, some of you might be having feelings of jealousy, envy or something else unproductive. You need to STOP! The lesson to be learned here is to change your mindset and habits so you can take advantage of the tax laws just as Mitt and many other investors do.

Many of the clients I work with argue they cannot invest like Mitt Romney or Warren Buffet because these big-time investors have millions and millions of dollars to invest. This mindset is wrong!

It's true that the wealthy have a lot of money to invest, but it's irrelevant if you have $100, $1,000, $10,000, $100,000, or $1,000,000 to invest because the tax treatment is the same. Your goal as an investor is to have your money generate as much income as possible without you being there. You can start with small dollar amounts to invest, take the money generated from these investments, and keep investing it. Over time, you'll make more money and have it taxed at a lower rate, which will help you reach your financial freedom faster.

You can invest your money yourself or hire someone, such as a Certified Financial Planner (CFP) or Financial Advisor, to help you make investments. I encourage you to talk to a professional before proceeding with investing because of the risks involved.

Landlord

The second group of people own rental properties. Owning a rental property is one of the best strategies available for tax purposes. It's also favorable from an investor's perspective, because you can use other people's money to purchase and own the property. When you purchase a rental property, you can put down as little money as possible and use the bank's money to make up the difference.

Furthermore, rental income from a tenant can be used to pay your rental expenses. Rental expenses can include mortgage interest, property taxes, insurance, and homeowners association (HOA) fees. As a landlord, your goal is for rental income to meet or exceed your expenses.

Download a copy of the "Form 1040 Schedule E" from the Internet as a reference. You only need page 1 of the schedule. The Schedule E is used to report rental activities for the year. It gets attached to the Form 1040.

The property address, the type of property, and the number of days rented is reported on top of the form. Then total rental income received for the year is reported. Many people think that all of the rental income is taxed. This is untrue. Only your net income from a rental is taxed. Net income is calculated as the rents received minus all of the expenses paid during the year.

Remember all of those expenses I mentioned in Chapter 2 that you don't get to write off when you live in a home as your personal residence? You can write them off for a rental property!

Review the list of expenses listed on the Schedule E. You're allowed to write off any ordinary and necessary expenses related to the rental property. Note that the principal portion of your mortgage payment is not deductible, only the mortgage interest portion is.

Even if you have a small profit after paying rental expenses, you may have an overall loss due to depreciation. Depreciation for tax purposes is the allocation of the cost of an asset to periods in which the asset is used. For residential property, such as a single-family residence or a condominium, a portion of the total cost of the property would be depreciated each year over 27.5 years, per the tax laws. For commercial property, such as a shopping center or an office building, a portion of the costs would be depreciated each year over 39 years, per the tax laws.

For tax purposes, you can only depreciate the portion allocable to the structure. You can't depreciate the land portion of real estate. Talk to a real estate appraiser to get the exact land to structure ratio for your property.

There is no cash outlay for depreciation, but there is a tax benefit. The benefit is that the depreciation on your tax return can reduce taxable rental income. Even if you're cash flow positive each month after expenses, depreciation could reduce your net profit to zero or generate a loss. A loss may reduce your AGI and result in lower taxes. This is how landlords pay no taxes on a portion of the money they make each year.

If you actively participate in the rental activity, you can take up to $25,000 in rental losses (passive losses) against your other income (nonpassive income), such as your wages. Active participation means that you own at least 10% of the rental property and you make management decisions, such as approving tenants, deciding on rental terms, or arranging for repairs.

Scenario

- ✧ Your annual wages are $100,000
- ✧ You purchase a rental property for $200,000
- ✧ The structure is worth 60% of the total costs, which is $120,000
- ✧ Rental income is $1,000 a month
- ✧ Rental expenses are $850 a month

Depreciation

Depreciation is $4,363 a year, or $363 a month.

$$\frac{120,000 \ value \ of \ structure}{27.5 \ years} = \$4,363 \ depreciation \ per \ year$$

Net Profit or Loss

	Per Month	**Per Year**
Rental Income	$1,000	$12,000
Rental Expenses	-$850	-$10,200
Tentative Net Income (Excess Cash Flow)	$150	$1,800
Depreciation	-$363	-$4,363
Net Loss (Tax Benefit)	**-$213**	**-$2,563**

Excess Cash Flow

Your monthly rental income of $1,000 a month exceeds your monthly expenses of $850 by $150. This excess $150 can be used to pay towards the principal of the loan on the property or to supplement your income.

Tax Benefit

Your yearly loss of $2,563 calculated above can be taken against your wages to lower your AGI and taxable income. This is an awesome benefit because you didn't spend $2,563 to get this loss. You got this loss on your tax return due to a tax deduction allowed for depreciating the structure that you purchased with borrowed money. That's right! You borrowed the bank's money to purchase the home, yet you're able to write off the depreciation on your tax return. This clearly shows how the rich get richer by using other people's money!

These amounts would look like this on a tax return.

Income	7	Wages, salaries, tips, etc. Attach Form(s) W-2	7	100,000
	8a	Taxable interest. Attach Schedule B if required	8a	
Attach Form(s) W-2 here. Also attach Forms W-2G and 1099-R if tax was withheld.	b	Tax-exempt interest. Do not include on line 8a ... 8b		
	9a	Ordinary dividends. Attach Schedule B if required	9a	
	b	Qualified dividends ... 9b		
	10	Taxable refunds, credits, or offsets of state and local income taxes	10	
	11	Alimony received	11	
	12	Business income or (loss). Attach Schedule C or C-EZ	12	
If you did not get a W-2, see instructions.	13	Capital gain or (loss). Attach Schedule D if required. If not required, check here ▶ ☐	13	
	14	Other gains or (losses). Attach Form 4797	14	
	15a	IRA distributions . 15a b Taxable amount	15b	
	16a	Pensions and annuities 16a b Taxable amount	16b	
Enclose, but do not attach, any payment. Also, please use Form 1040-V.	17	Rental real estate, royalties, partnerships, S corporations, trusts, etc. Attach Schedule E	17	-2,563
	18	Farm income or (loss). Attach Schedule F	18	
	19	Unemployment compensation	19	
	20a	Social security benefits 20a b Taxable amount	20b	
	21	Other income. List type and amount	21	
	22	Combine the amounts in the far right column for lines 7 through 21. This is your total income ▶	22	97,437

There is one major hurdle to deducting rental losses against your other income. Once your income exceeds $100,000, the $25,000 special allowance is reduced by 50 cents for every dollar above $100,000 and is completely phased out when your income reaches $150,000. In other words, once your income exceeds $150,000, you can't deduct any of your rental losses against your other income (nonpassive income) for that year. This is the same if you file married filing jointly or as single. There's a marriage penalty for you!

For instance, if you make $80,000 a year as a salary and file single, you could deduct your rental losses against your wages. If you get married and your spouse also makes $80,000 a year, your combined income filing jointly is $160,000, which exceeds $150,000, so you cannot deduct any of your rental losses against your wages. If you both have rental properties with losses and your combined income puts you over the $150,000 threshold, is it worth getting married?

Many clients I work with argue that rentals aren't a good strategy for them because their income is greater than

$150,000 and they cannot deduct the rental losses each year. I tell them to stop thinking this way! That's how non-rich people think. They think day-to-day, month-to-month, year-to-year, which is short-term. Rich people don't think like this. They think 5 years later, 10 years later, 15 years later, 20 or more years later, which is more long-term.

If you're able to have excess money each month from your rental income being greater than your rental expenses, and none of this money is taxed now because of the depreciation deduction, you're still coming out ahead. The trick is to keep duplicating this and own multiple rental properties so you can have more monthly income that is nontaxed.

Plus, over time, you're acquiring an asset that might appreciate in value. You could sell the property for a gain in which part of the gains would be taxed at the long-term capital gains rate if you own it over a year. You could avoid tax by deferring any taxable gains if you exchange the property for a similar property in a like-kind exchange, also known as a Section 1031 Exchange. You could gift the property to a family member or friend. You could donate it to a charity. You could leave it to your estate so your beneficiaries could inherit it. There are many things you could do because now you have an asset that didn't require a lot of your money to acquire and maintain.

Don't be discouraged that losses are not deductible in a current year if your income is over $150,000. Any loss not allowed in a current year is suspended. That means that you don't lose it. You can claim a suspended loss later when (1) your income falls below $150,000, (2) you have passive income from other rentals, or (3) you sell the property. Rich people love that last point because they understand that even though they didn't get a deduction each year for their rental losses, they get to claim the suspended losses from these rentals when they sell the property years later, thereby minimizing any tax on the gain. They understand that claiming the rental losses is just a timing difference. They were unable to take advantage of the loss in years one through five, but were able to claim all of the suspended losses when they sold the property in year six.

Talk to a tax professional for more information on this strategy. You can also review Publication 17 on the IRS's website at www.irs.gov for more information.

Small Business Owner

The third group is comprised of small business owners. Business owners have the biggest advantage over employees because the tax laws are written in their favor. Remember, it's the rich who are influencing tax laws and many of them are business owners.

Employee

Let's assume you make $100,000 a year in wages as an employee. When you work for an hour, who gets paid first? Is it you? No, it's the government. The IRS and the state taxing agency, depending on the state you work in, get paid before you do through the taxes that are taken out of your pay.

On a $100,000 salary, if you filed as single and claimed the standard deduction in 2013, you would end up with approximately $66,456 after paying federal income taxes, Social Security taxes, Medicare taxes, state income taxes (California taxes used in this example), and any other local and/or state taxes (California State Disability Insurance used in this example). In other words, 34% of your hard earned money goes to taxes and you get the benefit of 66% of your $100,000 salary. This only gets worse as you make more money.

Salary	$100,000	
Federal Income Taxes*	-$18,500	
CA State Income Taxes	-$6,394	
Social Security Taxes	-$6,200	
Medicare Taxes	-$1,450	
CA State Disability Insurance	-$1,000	
Total Taxes	-$33,544	*34%*
Income Remaining After Taxes	$66,456	*66%*
Single filing status and standard deduction		

Ask yourself, if this was your situation, how much money would you have left over after paying your bills and trying to save for financial freedom? For many Americans, this is a major problem.

Business Owner

Business owners don't have this problem because they pay themselves first and then pay taxes to the government. When a business owner sells a product or service, the money is not taxed at this level. The business owner first gets to deduct expenses against the sales and then is taxed on the profit. If there is a loss, there is no tax. This is similar to the treatment of net income from a rental property.

To illustrate, go to the Internet, do a search for "Form 1040 Schedule C" and download this form. The Schedule C has two pages. The Schedule C is used to report a sole proprietor's business activities for the year. It gets attached to the Form 1040.

On this schedule, you report the information about your business, such as your name, the business name, explanation of business, and address. Then you report all of your sales, also known as gross receipts, and any ordinary and necessary expenses for the business. You must report all of your sales you made in a year.

Next, deduct expenses against income to decrease your taxable profit. The expenses listed on the Schedule C are not all inclusive. The Schedule C only lists some of the more common expenses for a business.

The biggest tax advantage of being a business owner versus an employee is that business owners are allowed to convert personal expenses into legal business deductions if those expenses are considered ordinary and necessary expenses related to the operation of the activity. This includes, but is not limited to, a home office, vehicle, meals and entertainment, travel, computer, cell phone bill, and gifts. For this reason, a business owner having $100,000 in sales will pay less tax than an employee with a salary of $100,000, assuming all other factors are equal.

Let's look at a scenario in which you provide a service as an independent contractor or freelancer (business owner) with sales of $100,000. We'll compare this to you being an employee providing the same service and earning a salary of $100,000. Your expenses mentioned below are $20,000 regardless if you're a business owner or an employee. These are the hypothetical personal expenses you can convert into legal business deductions.

	Business Owner	**Employee**
Salary		$100,000
Sales	$100,000	
Personal Expenses Converted to Legal Business Deductions	-$20,000	$0
Net Profit	$80,000	$100,000
Taxes:		
Federal Income Taxes*	*$12,010*	*$18,500*
CA State Income Taxes	*$4,004*	*$6,394*
Social Security & Medicare Tax (Self-Employment Tax)	*$11,304*	*$7,650*
CA State Disability Insurance	*$0*	*$1,000*
Total Taxes	-$27,318 27%	-$33,544 34%
Personal Expenses	$0	-$20,000
Total Income Remaining	$52,682 53%	$46,456 46%
*Single filing status and standard deduction		

As shown above, as a business owner you're able to legally convert the $20,000 in personal expenses into business deductions to decrease the amount that is taxed. As an employee, you're unable to deduct personal expenses. As a result, your taxes are lower and your remaining income is greater as a business owner. The benefit increases as you're able to deduct more expenses.

As a business owner, only 27% of your hard-earned money goes to taxes and you have 53% of your income remaining after taxes and expenses. As an employee, 34% of your hard-earned money goes to taxes and you have 46% of your income remaining after taxes and expenses.

This example shows you how an employee doing the same work as a business owner for the same pay will end up paying more in tax. That's why it's more advantageous to be a business owner from a tax perspective. Our tax laws are the most complex in the world and this example was just for illustrative purposes to prove a point. If you decide to become a business owner, I highly recommend you work with a tax advisor and other professionals to ensure you're in compliance with the tax laws.

Another major advantage that self-employed people have over employees is self-employed people can contribute more to retirement accounts. This is more advantageous for people who expect to be in a lower tax bracket when they withdraw the money. Employees can contribute up to a certain amount into a retirement account, such as a 401(k) or 403(b). For 2013, the maximum amount an employee could contribute to his or her own 401(k) or 403(b) was $17,500. This maximum amount could be increased each year based on the tax laws.

In addition to the employee's contribution to the retirement account, the employee's employer could contribute to the employee's retirement account as a matching or profit sharing contribution. A matching contribution is when an employer matches an employee's contribution to a retirement account up to a certain percentage of the employee's salary, which is typically between 1% and 5% of the employee's salary. A profit sharing contribution is when an employer contributes to an employee's retirement account an amount that is based on a set formula for determining how it'll be divided among employees. It's common for this contribution formula to be based on a percentage of the employee's salary, which is typically between 1% to 5%. The employer's contributions, if any, are in addition to the employee's contributions.

Having your employer make a contribution to your retirement account sounds good, but most employers are not making large contributions, if they're even doing it at all, due to costs. As a result, employees typically can only get up to their own contribution limits of $17,500 for 2013.

A self-employed person does not have this limitation depending on how his or her company is structured. To continue with our example from before, if you had a profit of $80,000 from your business, you could contribute to your 401(k) both as an employee and as an employer, even though you're not really an employee of your own sole proprietorship. In 2013, with a profit of $80,000, you could personally contribute up to $17,500 as an employee and you could have a profit sharing plan to contribute up to $14,870 as an employer for a total of $32,370.

> $17,500 Employee Contribution
> + $14,870 Profit Sharing
> = $32,370 Total

As a self-employed person, the amount of your employer's profit sharing plan contribution is calculated as a percent of your profit. For 2013, the maximum you could contribute combined as an employee and employer was $51,000.

Self-employed people have a huge advantage over employees because they have an opportunity to contribute more to a retirement account on the same amount of money and lower their taxes currently because the contributions are pre-tax. In our example above, if you were self-employed, you could contribute an additional $14,870 to your 401(k) on the same amount of income as if you were an employee. The wealthy are able to make large pre-tax contributions to their retirement accounts and withdraw the money when they're in a lower tax bracket. No wonder the rich are getting richer!

Setting up a retirement account to take advantage of this strategy must be done correctly so I encourage you to engage a competent professional.

Chapter Summary

To reach your financial freedom faster, you need to change the way you make your money. Focus your energy on (1) investing, (2) being a landlord, and/or (3) owning a small business.

When you look at your tax return, where is most of your income coming from? If it's wages, you need to make a change now! Circled below is where you need to generate more income on your tax return, Form 1040.

Income				
	7	Wages, salaries, tips, etc. Attach Form(s) W-2		7
	8a	**Taxable** interest. Attach Schedule B if required		8a
Attach Form(s) W-2 here. Also attach Forms W-2G and 1099-R if tax was withheld.	b	Tax-exempt interest. **Do not** include on line 8a . . .	8b	
	9a	Ordinary dividends. Attach Schedule B if required		9a
	b	Qualified dividends	9b	
	10	Taxable refunds, credits, or offsets of state and local income taxes		10
	11	Alimony received		11
If you did not get a W-2, see instructions.	12	Business income or (loss). Attach Schedule C or C-EZ		12
	13	Capital gain or (loss). Attach Schedule D if required. If not required, check here ▶ ☐		13
	14	Other gains or (losses). Attach Form 4797		14
	15a	IRA distributions .	15a	b Taxable amount . . .	15b
	16a	Pensions and annuities	16a	b Taxable amount . . .	16b
Enclose, but do not attach, any payment. Also, please use Form 1040-V.	17	Rental real estate, royalties, partnerships, S corporations, trusts, etc. Attach Schedule E		17
	18	Farm income or (loss). Attach Schedule F		18
	19	Unemployment compensation		19
	20a	Social security benefits	20a	b Taxable amount . . .	20b
	21	Other income. List type and amount		21
	22	Combine the amounts in the far right column for lines 7 through 21. This is your **total income** ▶		22

- CHAPTER 5 -

Challenges

Becoming an investor, landlord, or small business owner is an achievable goal – though not an easy one. If it was easy, everyone would do it. Understanding the challenges of each path is an important factor in considering which path works best for you.

Becoming an Investor

1. Money to Invest

Having money to invest is the biggest challenge to becoming an investor. Many of the clients I work with tell me they are barely able to pay their bills and have no money left over to invest. I believe most people should be able to save a small amount of money by cutting back on unnecessary expenses. For example, it's not necessary to buy coffee, smoothies, or lunch every day, or go out to eat dinner several times a week. Splurging on these niceties once in a while is okay, but there's always room to cut cost here and save money. Ask yourself if you really need to go on that extravagant vacation or drive a luxury car. Would a modest vacation and a more economical car be sufficient?

The trick to investing is to understand that it's not about how much you make; it's about how much money you have remaining after paying all of your necessary bills. Fortunately, you can start investing with as little as $100.

2. Fear of Losing Money

It's difficult enough to save money to invest, but it's even harder to accept that you might lose your money. With investing, there's a justifiable fear that you could lose money on your investment. In my opinion, this is a realistic challenge of becoming an investor, whereas not being able to save money is an unrealistic challenge.

It's irrelevant what investment you choose because they all have the risks of decreasing in value. The investments that have less risk tend to have lower financial returns; likewise, investments with more risk tend to have higher financial returns.

For instance, a savings account has low risk because it's insured by the government. The government, through the FDIC (Federal Deposit Insurance Corporation), guarantees the safety of your money up to $250,000. As a result, the return on this investment, or interest earned, is very low. Alternatively, owning stock in a company may generate higher returns, but the risk increases substantially because it's not insured.

3. Selecting the Best Investments

If you want to become wealthy by being an investor, you need to choose investments that will generate a financial return on your principal. The complexity and uncertainty of the stock market, bond market, or any other investment market makes it very difficult to pick good investments.

Many things impact the investment market. This includes, but is not limited to, supply and demand of an investment, hype, government regulations, economic trends, inflation, interest rates, natural catastrophes, and world events, such as war. Even if you read investment books, research an investment thoroughly, and feel in your heart and mind that an investment is good, there is no guarantee that it'll be a good investment.

4. Finding a Suitable Financial Advisor

If you decide not to pick investments on your own, you can hire a financial advisor for guidance. How would you go about finding a good financial advisor? Just like trying to find any good service provider, such as an attorney, doctor, or tax preparer, the task is daunting.

There are many different types of financial professionals, including Certified Financial Planner (CFP), Chartered Financial Analyst (CFA), and Certified Public Accountant (CPA) with a Personal Financial Specialist (PFS) designation. It's not advisable to choose a professional based solely on his or her designation. Make sure he or she has experience with your issue. You need to like working with the person and trust his or her judgment. You also have to determine which fee structure he or she offers, such as a fee-only basis, a percentage of assets under management, or a commission on each transaction.

Although the process of hiring a good financial advisor is very difficult, there are plenty of resources to guide you through the process. You can do a search on the Internet for "how to find a good financial advisor" for more information. Learn what the different professional designations mean and how the different fee structures work. Talk to friends, family members, and professionals, such as an attorney or CPA, to see if they can provide you with names of reputable financial advisors. Chapter 8 includes more information about trusted advisors.

5. Success of the Financial Advisor

Even with a financial advisor, there's still a risk that you can lose money. A good financial advisor faces the same risks and challenges in the investment market that you would face if you invested your own money. The only difference is that financial advisors typically have more education and expertise with investment strategies. You're paying the financial advisor to use his or her skills to maximize your financial return. However, there are no guarantees.

It's common in the investment industry to use benchmarks to gauge how well a financial advisor is doing. A common benchmark is the S&P 500 index, which is Standard and Poor's list of 500 large companies having common stock listed on the New York Stock Exchange or NASDAQ. This index is generally a reflection of how well the entire U.S.

stock market is doing. People also use it to judge the performance of the U.S. economy.

Most people outside of the investment industry do not
know that the S&P 500 index can be used as a benchmark.
They're unaware of the exchange traded fund (ETF) called
SPDR S&P 500 (SPY). SPY tracks the performance of the
S&P 500, which is, in turn, the benchmark for the stock market. If you bought one share of SPY, your investment performance would match the stock market. Purchasing an ETF is
similar to buying stock.

Therefore, if you want to invest and earn returns as well
as the U.S. market, you can purchase SPY. If you want returns better than the market, use SPY as the benchmark to
gauge how well you're doing.

Scenario

Investment 1

- ✧ You purchased one share of SPY on January 1
  for $100

- ✧ Now, on December 1 it's worth $150

The gain is $50.
$150 price now - $100 purchase price = $50 gain

The return is 50%.

$$\frac{\$50\ gain}{\$100\ purchase\ price} = 50\%\ return$$

Since SPY is the benchmark for the market, you can consider the market to have a 50% return during that time period.

Investment 2

✧ You purchase one share of XYZ Corporation on January 1 for $100

✧ Now, on December 1, it's worth $120

✧ The benchmark for the market is 50%, as determined above

The gain is $20.

$120 price now - $100 purchase price = $20 gain

The return is 20%.

$$\frac{\$20\ gain}{\$100\ purchase\ price} = 20\%\ return$$

Conclusion

Since SPY is the benchmark, you should have been able to earn at least a 50% rate of return in the same period. The return of 20% for XYZ Corporation is lower than the market, therefore, you did worse than the market.

Are you ready for some shocking news? Most financial advisors cannot beat the market. This means that in a given period, most financial advisors cannot invest solely in stocks and beat the market (S&P 500 index). The complexity of the stock market tests even the best financial advisor in consistently generating returns higher than the market.

My intention is not to downplay the value of financial advisors. It's simply to enlighten you that hiring a financial advisor doesn't guarantee a financial return. You could still lose money.

Asset Allocation

Most financial advisors suggest you use asset allocation to achieve your investment goals, which is to hold different assets because each asset performs differently in different markets and conditions. This diversification is supposed to reduce the risks of variability in returns.

For example, a financial advisor might suggest you hold some investments in stock, bonds, money market savings account, ETFs, gold, and foreign currency. What percentage of your total investment portfolio to hold in each type of asset depends on your age, risk tolerance, and financial goals.

Understand the risks associated with investing and proceed with caution. I encourage you to talk to a professional to help you achieve your financial goals. Read Chapter 8 about how to pick a trusted advisor.

Becoming a Landlord

1. Money for a Down Payment

If you want to become a landlord, you're going to need at least one rental property. A rental property can be a residential property, such as a single-family residence or a condominium, or a commercial property, such as a shopping center or an office building.

Many of the clients I work with tell me they don't have enough money to save for a down payment to purchase a rental property. This is the same challenge faced when becoming an investor. It's a challenge that can typically be overcome through discipline and sacrifice.

The price of the rental property and the amount of loan you qualify for determine how much of a down payment you'll need to purchase a rental property. Typically, you need to put down 20% of the cost and the bank will lend you the difference. I'm confident if you really want to purchase a rental property, you can cut costs and save money to come up with a down payment. The money you're saving has already been taxed, therefore, your goal is to put down as little money as possible and have the bank finance the rest.

If you currently own your home, another option is to move out of your personal residence and convert it into a rental. This will provide you with a rental property while you live somewhere else. Talk with a tax professional to learn more about this.

2. Finding Good Tenants Quickly

A lot of clients I work with have rental properties. Half of them love being a landlord and the other half hate being a landlord. The common theme with our clients who love being a landlord is that they have been able to quickly find good tenants.

If your property is vacant, you'll have to pay rental expenses out of your own pocket. A vacant property can strain your cash flow, but don't rush to find a tenant. Bad tenants typically pay late or damage your property. In extreme cases, you may need to take legal actions to evict them.

A good tenant is someone who pays on time, takes care of your property, and is easy to deal with. Fortunately, you can take steps to improve your chances of finding a good tenant, such as running a credit check, examining their payment history on bills, verifying their employment, and calling references.

3. Repairs and Improvements

If you're fortunate enough to buy a modern rental property then you might not have a lot of repairs and improvements. However, if you buy an older property, the chance of having to spend money on repairs and improvements increases. These costs could prevent you from having a positive cash flow from the property. The worst part about repairs and improvements is that you typically don't know when they'll be needed and how much they'll cost. This challenge can be overcome by saving money in advance to pay for repairs or improvements.

4. Liability

When you're a landlord, you subject yourself to the risk of being sued by your tenant. You could get sued for many reasons, including, but not limited to, not following state and/or city laws, failure to provide a safe, proper living environment, refusal to make repairs or improvements, disregard for the tenant's right to privacy, and unjustly keeping the tenant's security deposit.

Keeping the tenant's security deposit is the most common reason why a landlord is sued by their tenant. A landlord typically keeps a security deposit to pay for any damage to the rental property done by the tenant. The landlord's determination of the costs of the damage is subjective. Consequently, this could lead to conflict between the landlord and tenant, during which the tenant can sue the landlord for return of the security deposit.

You can protect yourself by having a good tenant, following the proper landlord-tenant state and city laws, and having proper insurance. If you want to become a landlord, I strongly advise you to hire an attorney to handle legal actions.

5. Uncertainty about the Property's Future Value

A major challenge to owning a rental property is the uncertainty regarding the property's future value. The great recession in 2008 showed that the price of a home can substantially decrease in value.

Many of the clients I work with use this as a reason to not purchase a rental property. I counter their concern by explaining that they only spent a down payment of 20% or less to purchase the rental property and the bank put up the rest of the money. The tenant is paying their monthly expenses, including the mortgage payment. There's only a slim chance that the value of the property will decrease below the down payment amount. Even if the property value did decrease below their down payment, they could continue to rent the property out to recoup their down payment. Another option is to sell the property and take a loss on their tax return against their other income.

Becoming a landlord has its challenges; consequently, you must understand the risks and proceed with caution. I encourage you to talk to professionals, such as an attorney, mortgage broker, real estate agent, appraiser, and home inspector.

Becoming a Small Business Owner

1. Funding a Venture

Similar to needing money to invest with or use as a down payment on a rental property, you may need money to start a company. As I mentioned before, most people are able to save money by reducing their personal expenditures. Three common ways to fund a venture are through your own savings; loans from friends, family, credit cards, and/or a bank; and investors. Many small businesses are funded through a combination of savings, credit cards, and loans from friends and family.

Funding a venture through an investor involves selling an ownership interest in your company. An investor is different than a lender. With a lender, you keep the ownership of your business, but have to repay the money. With an investor, you don't have to repay the money, but you give up some ownership. Investors risk losing their money if your business doesn't succeed.

Crowdfunding has become a popular way for people to obtain money to start a business. It's a collective effort of people who pool their money to support the efforts of another person or organization. Money can be raised through donations or selling equity. Donation crowdfunding is commonly used for disaster relief or political campaigns, but can also be used for funding a startup company or new product development.

Equity crowdfunding involves raising money by selling ownership of a company to investors. The government regulates this type of funding so I recommend you talk to a professional, such as an attorney, CPA, or business broker, before pursuing this option. You can learn more by doing a search on the Internet for the term "crowdfunding" and researching crowdfunding companies.

Most of the time it takes money to start a business, but don't let that hold you back. If you truly believe in your business idea, you'll find a way to fund your venture. A combination of savings, loans, money from investors, and money from crowdfunding can help you get started. If finding the funds to start a business is a major obstacle for you, consider starting a service business. Many service businesses, such as a consulting company or dog walking business, typically require very little or no money to start up.

2. Having a Business Idea to Make a Profit

Many of the clients I work with say that they have money to start a business, but they don't have a profitable business idea. This is a common concern. Fortunately, you don't need a groundbreaking idea to succeed. However, you do need a profit motive to start a business. A profit motive means you strive to sell a product or service to generate income that exceeds your business expenses. Chapter 6 includes more information on how to start your venture.

3. Ability to Sell

Generating enough sales or revenue is the most important and challenging aspect of running a successful business. You can have the best product or service in the whole world, but if you can't sell it, you'll go out of business.

Many people think that successful salespeople were born with a natural gift for sales. This is not true! Anyone can learn how to sell. Selling is a skill that can be learned, but just like any other skill, you need to be educated on the subject. You also need to continuously practice what you learned. To gain and/or improve your sales skills, you can take classes, read books, and talk to friends or family members who are salespeople. Don't let the lack of a sales background hold you back from starting your venture.

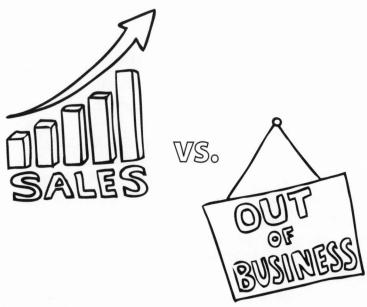

4. Multiple Business Functions

Running a successful business involves more than just sales. It involves a wide variety of business functions, including: accounting, computer systems maintenance, sales, marketing, human resources, management, and strategic planning. Unfortunately, these responsibilities become distractions. Business owners get caught up in the daily activities of running a business and neglect to focus on making a profit. This can lead to failure despite strong sales.

It's important to keep control of expenses to improve your profitability. Generating a profit will make the venture worthwhile and sustainable. Improve your chances of success by seeking advice from professionals and educating yourself on strategies to run a business efficiently and effectively.

5. Time

There are many opportunity costs involved when starting a business. An opportunity cost is the loss of a potential benefit from one option when another option is chosen. The largest opportunity cost for most business owners is time. Time is your most valuable asset and must be used wisely. Once you use it, you can't get it back. Unlike investment or rental properties, businesses require a significant portion of your time.

As a business owner, your time spent with family and friends will be severely impacted. You may be accustomed to eating dinner with your family every night. However, as a business owner, you may have to work late into the evening and miss dinner. The opportunity cost is the family time you're giving up in exchange for your commitment to the business.

Be aware that as a business owner, you'll have to make sacrifices. Only you can decide if you want to invest the time in a venture that'll help you reach financial freedom faster.

Best Choice

Each path to financial freedom has challenges. Some challenges are common among all three paths, but to a different extent. For instance, all three paths require some money upfront. However, purchasing a rental property requires large amounts of cash. Unexpected repairs and improvements to a rental property can be costly. You also need the cash flow to cover expenses during any time your property is vacant. Alternatively, a service company can be started with very minimal cash.

All three paths are risky. Investing, with or without a financial advisor, can be very risky. The biggest threat with investing is the uncertainty of the markets. You have no control over the volatility of the markets. Likewise, you have no control over the housing market. A severe downturn in the economy could hurt both the investment and housing markets significantly.

As a small business owner, you maintain control over your own products and/or services. You control the expenses related to running your business. You can't control the demand for your product or service, but you can adjust sales efforts and your business model to meet consumers' demands and needs.

All three paths have tax benefits. As an investor, your gains receive preferential tax treatment. Through depreciation, your rental property could generate a tax loss. The most significant tax benefits exist for small business owners, for they're able to convert their personal expenses into legal business deductions.

The immediate tax benefit available to landlords is limited by AGI thresholds. As discussed previously, their ability to write off rental losses is phased out if they make too much money. Business owners, on the other hand, can convert their personal expenses into legal business deductions without regard to income levels.

Some of the rich outsmart the system by incorporating a combination of investing, being a landlord, and owning a business. For example, they invest the money they save by being a business owner or they use their investment income to purchase rental properties. For these reasons, it's important to gain an understanding of all three paths.

Overall, most self-made millionaires in America are business owners. The remainder of this book will focus on starting a business and will reveal more secrets of the rich.

CHAPTER 6

Venture

Many of the richest Americans have made their wealth by being small business owners. By owning small businesses, they changed the way they earned their income and have taken advantage of the tax laws that favor small business owners. Through their businesses, the rich are able to convert personal expenses into legal business deductions. They're able to write off these expenses directly against business sales.

Many of today's well-known, successful businesses started small and grew to become some of the world's largest companies. For example, Amazon, Apple, Dell, Google, Harley-Davidson, Hewlett Packard, and Mattel all started in a garage.

Starting your own business venture has many challenges, some of which you learned about in the previous chapter. Don't let the challenges hold you back from starting a business. Life presents challenges to those who can handle them. Any obstacle you face in your life is meant for you and can be overcome. To be successful, direct your energy towards overcoming any challenge you face.

One common characteristic I've noticed among successful people I've met and researched is their skill at overcoming obstacles. The more challenges you face, the more opportunities you have to overcome them, and when you do, the more successful you will be. You can overcome the challenges of starting a business and, in turn, reach financial freedom faster.

If you want to start your own business, do it! Don't worry about the critics who say you can't do it or hold you back in any other fashion. The critics will always be there. Their negative energy will keep them in their current element, never knowing success or failure, but always wondering. The credit will always belong to you because you took the risk to start your own venture and overcame challenges as they arose.

Even if you fail at being a business owner, at least you tried and will know what it's like. Everything you do today better prepares you for the future, no matter what the future brings. You'll learn more from failure than anything else. Each failure puts you closer to success, so take the risk.

You might be wondering if you can start your business in addition to your current full-time job. The answer is yes! The tax law doesn't say that you can't have a side business while working at another job, but you must have a profit motive for your business. Profit motive is discussed in more detail throughout this chapter. You can keep your job to ensure money is coming in as you start your business. This is a great way to do it!

While maintaining a profitable business can be challenging, starting the business isn't that difficult to do. In most parts of the nation, there is little or no licensing requirements and you can operate your business out of your home with very little costs. Contact a professional, such as an attorney or CPA, for more guidance.

There are many steps you can take to help your business be successful, including, but not limited to, writing a business plan, developing a marketing plan, doing market research, forming an entity, and finding a mentor. Many books, classes, and seminars can teach you the necessary steps to start a successful business. Keep in mind that although these actions improve your odds for success, there is, unfortunately, no guarantee that you'll be successful.

When starting your business, keep the big picture in mind. Don't get too hung up in the details. Remember to focus on selling and making a profit. I've seen too many businesses fail because the owners got bogged down with the details. For example, some owners spent too much time on perfecting their business plans. Other owners overspent on items that they didn't need yet, such as trademarks or advanced inventory systems. They were overly concerned with these details and lost focus on their goals. Again, your goal as a business owner is to make a profit.

Let's review the most important concepts for you to start your own business or make sure your current business is on the right track.

Product or Service

All businesses, of all sizes, around the whole world, primarily provide one of two things: (1) a product, such as a phone, or (2) a service, such as tax return preparation. Some businesses provide a combination of a product and service, such as a restaurant, although, they still primarily provide one or the other. Which do you think is easier to come up with to start your own business, a product or a service? You got it, a service! A service requires you to sell your skill, whereas a product requires you to sell a tangible item.

Creating a product on your own is difficult enough, but even if you do, you need to build a prototype and obtain a patent to protect others from stealing your idea. You also need to choose to either sell and manufacture the product yourself or license it to another company to manufacture and sell. The development of a product can be very daunting.

If you can't develop your own product, you can resell someone else's product online or in a retail store. Being a reseller has become very popular due to the online market. Many clients I work with sell a variety of items on the Internet, such as bikes, boat parts, books, clothes, purses, software applications, women's makeup, shoes, and sunglasses. Through this method, you can still focus on selling a product even if you can't invent your own.

Starting a business that provides a service is easier because it only requires your skill; you don't need to come up with your own product or sell someone else's product. Also, the costs to start a service business are typically less than that of a product business or a reseller business.

Start a Service Business Now

I strongly encourage all taxpayers, including you, to have your own service business. This will allow you to take advantage of the tax laws just as the rich do. It'll help you lower your taxes and enable you to reach financial freedom faster.

What service can you provide? You can provide any service you want. You can provide a service that is already being provided, or you can think of a unique service. I encourage you to first find something you love to do and then figure out a way to get paid for it. If you can't find something you love to do, find something you're good at that you can make money doing. The options are unlimited!

Below is a list of 50 different service businesses you can easily start:

Animal Breeding   *Dog Walking*
Artist   *Event Planning*
Babysitting or Nannying   *Filmmaking*
Bed and Breakfast   *Fitness Instruction*
Billing   *Gardening*
Bookkeeping   *Graphic Artist*
Car Washing and Detailing *Gun Instruction*
Carpet Cleaning   *Handyman*
Catering   *Holiday Wrapping*
Child-Care Providing   *Home Electronics Installation*
Cleaning   *Home Health Aid*
Computer Repair   *Interior Design*
Consulting   *Locksmith*
Delivery Service   *Mechanic*
Disk Jockey   *Network Marketing*

Personal Chef
Personal Shopping
Personal Training
Pet Grooming
Pet Sitting
Photography
Pool Cleaning
Power Washing
Private Investigation
Professional Speaking

Proofreading
Gift Basket Providing
Relocation Consultant
Resume Writing
Self-Defense Instruction
Tour Guide
Tutoring
Virtual Assistant
Web Design
Writing

The list above is not all inclusive. To find more ideas, you can do a search on the Internet or in books for types of service businesses you could start on your own.

Purpose and Differentiation

Your business must have a purpose. That purpose should be one of two things: (1) fill a need or (2) solve a problem. For example, a hairstylist is filling a need by cutting or styling someone's hair. A pharmaceutical company is constantly trying to create a new drug to cure a disease. If you focus your energy on one or both of these purposes, your venture will be on the track to success. If your business purpose is not one of these two things, your odds of success are lower.

Business Purpose = Fill a Need OR Solve a Problem

In addition to your business's purpose, it's essential to determine what differentiates your business from competitors. Examples of differentiation include providing better quality service, a lower price, more experience, a guarantee, or more innovative solutions. Your differentiation can be whatever you want; however, to ensure success it must align with your business purpose.

What is a mission statement?

A mission statement explains the purpose of a business. It is a clear, concise explanation of the intention of your business. Read more about creating a mission statement on the Internet.

Technical Skill and Sales Skill

Many people mistakenly think that providing a quality product or service is all that is required for success. In reality, the technical skill is only half of the equation. This is true regardless if you provide a product or service. For example, a software engineer may be able to develop an exceptional program. However, if he or she can't sell it, no one will know about it.

Sales are the lifeblood of your business. You need to make sales in order to be profitable and stay in business.

$$\begin{array}{r} \textit{Technical Skill} \\ \underline{+ \textit{Sales Skill}} \\ = \textit{Success} \end{array}$$

Your Goal is Profit

Your primary goal with a business venture is to make a profit. It's that simple. I tell every client I work with they should focus all of their energy on two things to ensure they're profitable. First, I explain they need to sell as much as they can. Second, I explain they need to keep their business costs as low as possible. No matter how high sales are, a business won't be profitable if expenses are higher. Don't be tempted to spend money just for the tax deduction if you really don't need the item or service you're purchasing. If you spend more money than you have coming in, you'll eventually be out of business.

Having a profit will ensure the livelihood of your business so you make more money and reach financial freedom faster. Profitability is also important so that the IRS doesn't view your activity as a hobby, as discussed below.

$$Sales$$
$$\underline{-\ Expense}$$
$$=\ Profit\ (Your\ Goal)$$

Always remain focused on making a profit, despite all the challenges you face and all the tasks you have to juggle.

Hobby vs. Business Activity

Although your goal as a business owner is to have a profit, it's common for a business in its first years to have a loss. The IRS scrutinizes businesses that have losses for too many years. If a business has too many losses, the IRS may determine that it's a hobby and not a business.

The IRS will presume your activity is carried on for profit if you make a profit at least three years out of the last five years (two years out of the last seven years if your activity consists of breeding, training, showing, or racing of horses).

If you don't have a profit three years out of the last five, then you have to prove your activity is for profit based on your facts and circumstances.

Even if your activity meets this three out of five years profits test, the IRS can challenge the profit motive presumption if the facts indicate that the activity isn't really a business because your profits are small compared to your large losses in other years. The good news is that if you meet this test, the activity is presumed to be for profit unless the government can show otherwise. This reduces the burden on you to prove your activity is for profit.

The IRS looks at the facts and circumstances of your activity to determine if it's a hobby or if it's a business activity engaged in for profit. The tax laws give nine factors for the IRS to consider when making this determination.

The nine relevant factors used to evaluate the profit motive of a business activity are:

1. Manner in which the taxpayer carries on the activity

2. Expertise of the taxpayer or his/her advisors

3. Time and effort expended by the taxpayer in carrying on the activity

4. Expectation that assets used in the activity may appreciate in value

5. Success of the taxpayer in carrying on other similar or dissimilar activities

6. Taxpayer's history of income or losses with respect to the activity

7. Amount of occasional profits, if any, which are earned

8. Financial status of the taxpayer

9. Elements of personal pleasure or recreation

You can read more about these factors on the Internet by doing a search for "Treasury Regulation Section 1.183-2" or "hobby versus business activity".

If the IRS concludes that your activity is not engaged in for profit, it can change your business activity to a hobby. This would disallow your loss from being taken against your other income, which results in an increase in taxable income and an increase in your tax liability.

Business losses are deductible against your other income, such as your wages, interest, and dividends. A business loss lowers your AGI, reduces your taxable income, and reduces your tax liabilities. Conversely, hobby losses are not deductible against your other income. If your business is determined to be a hobby, your tax liabilities will increase.

Remain focused on profitability. Make sure that your venture is engaged in a for-profit activity, because the IRS will be watching. Don't try to create a loss on your business tax return by only writing off expenses. This is a common issue audited by the IRS. If they audit this issue and you lose, you'll have to pay taxes, interest, and most likely penalties. It's not worth it. Talk to a tax professional to make sure you're on the right track.

Chapter Summary

All taxpayers, including you, should have a small business to take advantage of the tax laws like the rich do. Your business can sell either a product or service, but it's easier to start a service business because all it takes is a skill. Your business should fill a need or solve a problem. Differentiating your business from your competition will also help you make money.

Remember that just having a strong technical skill is not enough to be a successful business owner. You must also learn how to sell. At the end of each day, week, month, year, your only goal as a business owner is to make a profit. Always remember this and you'll be on the right track to being a successful business owner. In the next chapters, we're going to discuss the overall tax reporting requirements for your business.

CHAPTER 7

Tax Reporting

Understanding how to account for, track, and report your income and expenses will ensure you're on the right path for tax purposes. This is true for both new and existing business owners.

As a business owner, you can operate your venture as a sole proprietorship, partnership, or corporation. The tax laws for reporting your income and expenses, and maintaining your records, are the same for all of these entities. To illustrate this, we'll use the Form 1040 Schedule C (sole proprietorship) to explain the tax concepts, but please note that the concepts are the same for a partnership or corporation.

Please download a "Form 1040 Schedule C" from the Internet. This schedule has two pages and gets attached to your Form 1040. The Schedule C is used to report a sole proprietorship's business activities for the year. There are two main parts to this schedule. Income is reported in Part 1 and expenses are reported in Part 2. Your income minus expenses will determine if you have a profit or loss.

Accounting Method

There are two main accounting methods to report your income and expenses: (1) cash basis and (2) accrual basis.

Cash Basis

On a cash basis, you report sales or revenue as income when you receive a payment. For example, if you provide a service for a client on December 26 and your client doesn't pay you for the services you provided until January 3, you report the income on January 3. Expenses work in a similar fashion. You write off an expense when you pay it. Almost all small business owners, especially service providers, will use the cash basis of accounting.

Accrual Basis

On an accrual basis, you report sales or revenue as income when they're earned, not when payments are received. Likewise, you write off expenses when you incur them, not when you pay them. Using our previous example, you report the sale as income on December 26 because you earned the money at that time. Expenses are reported in a similar fashion. This method of accounting is required for large companies. Accrual basis reporting is complex and costly for taxpayers. Therefore, it's not common to see a small business on an accrual basis of accounting.

Going forward, we'll assume you're using the cash basis of accounting.

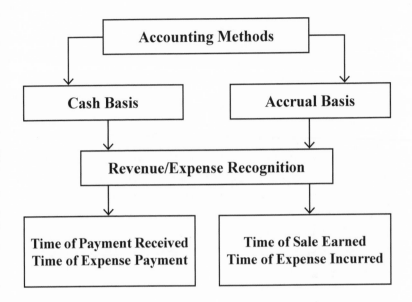

Income

The tax laws state that you must report all of your income. The total money you receive for selling a product or providing a service must be reported on Part 1 of the Schedule C.

The cost of goods sold section of Part 1 is where you report the cost of tangible items or products sold. Cost of goods sold subtracted from sales equals gross profit. Service providers typically don't sell any products, and therefore, don't have cost of goods sold.

Other income, such as awards, prizes, interest income, tax refunds, and scrap sales related to your business, are also reported on Part 1 of the Schedule C. This type of income, except for interest income, is not common for a business.

Part I	Income			
1	Gross receipts or sales. See instructions for line 1 and check the box if this income was reported to you on Form W-2 and the "Statutory employee" box on that form was checked . . . . ▶ ☐	1		
2	Returns and allowances	2		
3	Subtract line 2 from line 1	3		
4	Cost of goods sold (from line 42)	4		
5	**Gross profit.** Subtract line 4 from line 3	5		
6	Other income, including federal and state gasoline or fuel tax credit or refund (see instructions)	6		
7	**Gross income.** Add lines 5 and 6 . . . . ▶	7		

Your sales must be reported on your business tax return as gross income, not net income. For example, I audited a taxpayer who split any income his business received among four other people. In one year, his business had approximately $1 million of income, of which $200,000 was his portion. He incorrectly tried to report only $200,000 on his tax return. The correct way to report his income was to report the full $1 million as sales and deduct as an expense the $800,000 that was split among the other four people.

Have you ever heard of a celebrity going to jail for a tax related issue? It was most likely because that person didn't report all of his or her income. With all of my experience preparing tax returns and working at the IRS, the most important thing I can tell you is to report all of your income. Not reporting all of your income is considered fraud. If you get caught for fraud, you could have steep penalties asserted on you and you may face jail time.

Do you know how the IRS figures out if you're underreporting income? There are a variety of ways, but the simplest method is through a bank deposit analysis (BDA). This is where the IRS takes all of your bank statements and looks at all of the cash, online transfers, wire transfers, and check deposits going into your bank account. Then the IRS takes this number and compares it to the sales amount reported on your business tax return. If there is a material difference, you'll have some explaining to do!

You might think you're clever by not depositing the money into your bank account and instead using the money to fund a personal brokerage account or retirement account, or paying off debt, such as a credit card, mortgage, or student loans. The IRS can obtain your account statements and ask you where the money came from.

The government is good at following the money. The IRS has been around for over 100 years and has spent that time making sure taxpayers are paying their fair share of taxes. The IRS also has indirect methods of finding unreported income. These methods include the markup method, net worth method, sources and applications of funds method, and unit and volumes method. If the IRS suspects you're underreporting income, it can find it.

Underreporting your income is not worth it due to the steep penalties and the possible risk of going to jail. There are enough tax laws that you can legally take advantage of to decrease your tax liability. You can talk to a tax professional about additional ways to take advantage of the tax laws.

I'll say it one more time: report all of your income!

Expenses

As a business owner, you're allowed to deduct any expense that is ordinary and necessary. Determining what is ordinary and necessary is very subjective. Therefore, knowing what to deduct can be confusing at times.

If you think of writing off expenses from an investor's point of view, it'll help you understand what you can claim as being ordinary and necessary. To illustrate, let's hypothetically say that you and I start a partnership. You are a 50% owner only as an investor not working at the company and I'm a 50% owner and the only person working at the company. You receive 50% of the net profits of the business, and I receive the other 50%.

When it comes to running the business, I'm in charge of generating sales and paying expenses. If I write off too many expenses, the profit will decrease and you'll receive less money. As an investor, you want the profit to be as large as possible so you make more money. Therefore, I should only be writing off expenses that are ordinary and necessary for the business and nothing more.

For example, if I write off my personal car 100% for business, it would reduce the business's profit and decrease the amount of money you receive. I'd have to explain to you, the investor, why this is an ordinary and necessary business expense. If I can't prove to you that this expense is ordinary and necessary you would be unhappy with me because I took away part of your profits. Your profits would decrease due to an expense that I incurred.

Using the investor's point of view will help you determine if an expenses is ordinary and necessary. Since the government taxes you on your profit from the business, it can be viewed as if the IRS is a silent investor in your business, which is why the government only wants you writing off ordinary and necessary expenses and nothing more. Each time you take a deduction on your tax return for your business, see it from an investor's point of view and assume that you'll have to explain it at some point to the IRS or other tax agency. This will help ensure you're in compliance with the tax laws.

What specifically can you write off as a business deduction? Review Part 2 of the Schedule C for a list of common business expenses. This list is a good guideline, but it's not all-inclusive. There's a section to put "other" ordinary and necessary expenses that are not listed in Part 2 of the Schedule C.

Part II Expenses — Enter expenses for business use of your home only on line 30.

#	Item	Line	Amount	#	Item	Line	Amount
8	Advertising	8		18	Office expense (see instructions)	18	
9	Car and truck expenses (see instructions)	9		19	Pension and profit-sharing plans	19	
10	Commissions and fees	10		20	Rent or lease (see instructions):		
11	Contract labor (see instructions)	11		a	Vehicles, machinery, and equipment	20a	
12	Depletion	12		b	Other business property	20b	
13	Depreciation and section 179 expense deduction (not included in Part III) (see instructions)	13		21	Repairs and maintenance	21	
				22	Supplies (not included in Part III)	22	
				23	Taxes and licenses	23	
14	Employee benefit programs (other than on line 19)	14		24	Travel, meals, and entertainment:		
15	Insurance (other than health)	15		a	Travel	24a	
16	Interest:			b	Deductible meals and entertainment (see instructions)	24b	
a	Mortgage (paid to banks, etc.)	16a		25	Utilities	25	
b	Other	16b		26	Wages (less employment credits)	26	
17	Legal and professional services	17		27a	Other expenses (from line 48)	27a	
				b	Reserved for future use	27b	

Two Groups of Ordinary and Necessary Business Expenses

Think of your expenses as being grouped into two different categories. The first group of expenses consists of expenses that are clearly ordinary and necessary business expenses. These are 100% deductible. Examples of these expenses include advertising expenses, business insurance, supplies, and business taxes and licenses.

The second group consists of personal expenses, which can be converted into legal business deductions. Typically, these expenses are partially, but not fully, deductible on your tax return. Due to their complexity, these expenses are worth discussing in more detail.

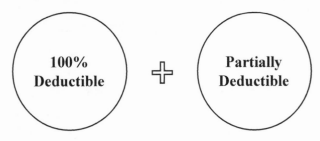

There are seven common partially deductible business expenses.

1. Home Office

If you have an area of your home that is used 100% for business, regularly and exclusively, and this is your only place of business, you can write off this portion of your home as a home office expense. The basics of the calculation are to take the square footage of your home that's used 100% for business divided by the total square footage of your home. This will give you a percentage. Multiply this percentage by all of your home expenses, such as mortgage interest, real estate taxes, insurance, rent, repairs and maintenance, and utilities.

Example

- ✧ Total square footage of your home is 2,000

- ✧ You use one bedroom, which is 200 square feet, 100% for business, regularly and exclusively, as your only place of business

- ✧ Total home expenses are $2,200 a month

You can write off 10% of your home expenses.

$$\frac{200\ sq.\ ft.\ home\ office}{2,000\ sq.\ ft.\ total} = 10\%$$

Your monthly home office deduction is $220 a month.

$2,200 monthly expenses x 10% = $220 monthly home office deduction

---

This calculation is a little complex so I encourage you to talk to a tax professional to ensure you're doing it right.

2. Vehicle

You're allowed to write off the cost of a car, van, or truck used for business purposes. You're required to keep a contemporaneous miles log. The miles log helps you prove what percentage your vehicle was used for business and for personal use. At the very least, it should show the following information:

Date	Destination *(City, Town, Area)*	Business Purpose	Business Miles	Expenses	
				Type (Gas, tolls, etc.)	Amount
		Total:		Total:	

Only the business miles or percentage is deductible. Commuting and other personal vehicle miles and expenses aren't deductible for business purposes.

There are two methods to write off your vehicle expenses: (1) actual expenses or (2) standard mileage deduction. You need to keep a miles log no matter which method you use.

If you use the actual expense method, you're required to keep track of all the actual expenses for your vehicle, such as gas, oil, repairs and maintenance, insurance, lease payments, and depreciation. This total is then multiplied by the business percentage you used your vehicle.

Alternatively, if you use the standard mileage deduction,

multiply the number of business miles you drove for the year by the rate the tax laws set each year. For 2013, the standard mileage rate was 56.5 cents per mile.

Example

✧ Total vehicle expenses for the year were $6,000

✧ You drove 10,000 miles total for the year

✧ 5,000 of those miles were for business

✧ Standard mileage rate for the year is 56.5 cents per mile

Actual Expenses
Business percentage equals 50%.

$$\frac{5,000 \text{ business miles}}{10,000 \text{ total miles}} = 50\% \text{ business use}$$

You would be able to deduct $3,000 on your tax return.

$6,000 vehicle expenses x 50% business use = $3,000

Standard Mileage
You would be able to write off $2,825 on your tax return.

5,000 business miles x 56.5 cents = $2,825

---

3. Meals and Entertainment

Meals and entertainment costs are deductible if they're directly related to, or associated with, the active conduct of your business. To prove the expenses were directly related to your business, you must show that the main purpose of the event was for business, you were engaged in business with a person during a meal or entertainment activity, and you have more than a general expectation of receiving income or some other benefit in the future. To prove the expenses were associated with your business, you must show these expenses were related to your business and occurred before or after a substantial business discussion. You're not required to devote more time to business than to entertainment.

These expenses include paying for meals and entertainment costs for a client, customer or employee. These costs can be for food, beverage, tax, tip, nightclubs, sporting events, hunting or fishing trips, or anything else you can claim as a meal or entertainment expense, but they cannot be lavish or extravagant.

Meals and entertainment expenses are only 50% deductible on your business tax return. You're allowed to write off these expenses related to your business. However, the government knows that there's an element of personal expenses so they only allow half of these expenses to be deducted.

To ensure you're in compliance with the tax laws, keep good records of who you met with, your relationship to this person, the business purpose, the location of where you met at, the number of people served, the date, and amount of the expense. Please see the recordkeeping section of this chapter for additional information.

4. Travel

Travel expenses away from your home for business are deductible. To keep it simple, away from home means that you sleep overnight on your business trip. Travel expenses include transportation, such as airplane, train, bus, and car rental, and meals and lodging.

To determine if any of your travel expenses are deductible or not depends on the facts and circumstances. The IRS will look at the amount of time you spent on personal activities compared to the amount of time you spent on activities related to the business.

If you're strictly away from home to visit with a client related to your business for one day and come right back home the next day, the travel expenses are entirely deductible. The tax laws clearly state if the entire cost of the trip was for personal reasons, such as vacation, you cannot deduct your travel expenses.

It's unclear if your travel expenses are deductible when your business trip is not entirely for business and is partially personal. If you have travel costs that are a mixture of business and personal, I recommend you keep the personal time you spend on the trip to a minimal and spend most of your time on business-related activities so you can claim the trip was primarily for business and write off the entire trip. If you're unsure, I suggest you only write off a portion of your travel costs related to the business trip. Writing off your travel expenses is not all or nothing. Only write off the travel expenses that are ordinary and necessary, and be ready to explain yourself to an IRS auditor.

If you started your trip primarily for business and then decided to extend your stay for a vacation, made a personal side trip, or had other personal activities, you can only deduct your business-related travel expenses.

5. Depreciable Assets

An asset is a tangible item that has a lifespan greater than a year. In other words, an asset can be used over a period of multiple years, not just one year. Examples of assets are your desktop computer, monitor, notebook, cell phone, camera, desk, and chair.

Since these assets can be used over one year, the tax laws require them to be depreciated. Depreciation for tax purposes is to allocate a portion of the total costs of an asset each year over a period while the asset was in use. For example, office furniture is typically depreciated over seven years, and computers and their peripheral equipment are typically depreciated over five years.

Any ordinary and necessary business expense is deductible. What about items that are used for both personally and in business? Only the portion of an item that is used 100% for business is deductible. This is a common issue for many small business owners.

For instance, if you purchase a new computer for $2,000 and you can reasonably estimate that you will only use it 60% of the time for business, you would only depreciate $1,200 of the cost for this new computer. The remaining $800 is not deductible because it's a personal expense.

You can use your best judgment to estimate what percentage you'll use an asset for business. From a former IRS auditor's perspective, backing out a portion of the total cost of an asset for personal use is better than backing out nothing. If you're in doubt as to what percentage to claim as the business portion, you could keep track of the time you spend using an asset for business and personal use for a week and then use this percentage.

6. Cell Phone

Almost all of my business clients I help have asked me if they can write off their cell phone bill each month. Have you ever wondered this? You're allowed to write off any expense that is ordinary and necessary. I'm confident that you don't use your one and only cell phone 100% for business, but you can write off the portion used for business and you can use your best judgment to determine what percentage that is. I only encourage you to be conservative in the amount you deduct. If you want to be exact, then you could trace each minute on your cell phone bill, but for the amount of the deduction, tracking each minute is probably not worth your time and interest.

7. Gifts

You're allowed to deduct up to $25 per person, per year for a business gift you give him or her. Any amount over the $25 is not deductible. Incidental costs to the gift, such as engraving, packaging, insuring, and mailing are not included with this limitation. This deduction is small, but it's still a good way to deduct expenses you incur for being generous.

For all of your expenses, I strongly encourage you to talk to a tax professional to make sure you're deducting your expenses correctly in accordance to the tax laws.

Net Profit or Loss

Review page 1 of the Schedule C. Income is reported in Part 1 and expenses are reported in Part 2. Your profit or loss is calculated at the bottom of the Schedule C on page 1. This amount is then reported on the front of your Form 1040 on line 12 and on the Schedule SE on line 2.

Any profit from your business is subject to three taxes on the Form 1040. Your business profit, reported on line 12 of the Form 1040, is used in calculating your federal income tax. In addition, it's subject to Social Security and Medicare taxes, which are collectively called self-employment tax. Self-employment tax is reported on Schedule SE, line 5, and on the Form 1040, page 2, line 56. Your profit will also be subject to state income taxes, depending on where you live and engage in business activity.

The taxes previously mentioned related to your business are only applied against profits. If you have a loss from your business, there will be no taxes on this business loss. Any loss from your business is still reported on the front of your Form 1040 on line 12. This loss reduces your taxable income, which could reduce your taxes.

The IRS is on the lookout for taxpayers who have losses from their business. Remember, a business loss is deductible against your other income, such as your wages, interest, and dividends. If the IRS determines your activity is a hobby, it'll disallow the loss from being taken against your other income. Without the loss, your taxable income would increase, thereby increasing your tax liability.

Recordkeeping

Based on my experience, the taxpayers who were the most organized with their records paid the least in taxes because they were able to account for all of their income and expenses. Therefore, it's crucial you understand how to maintain your tax records correctly.

You have the burden of proof to substantiate any sales or expense number that's reported on your tax return. As a result, you're required by law to maintain books and records to prove your income and expenses.

Bookkeepers and software developers fool business owners into believing they need to hire an expensive book-keeper or purchase a complex accounting program. I'm here to tell you that this isn't true. Surprisingly, keeping track of your income and expenses for tax purposes is really easy. It's basic math, adding and subtracting. If you can do math, you can maintain your own books and records.

You can keep your books and records in any manner that works for you so long as it clearly reflects your income (profit or loss). You could use a spreadsheet program or a word processor program on your computer, or even hand-write your transactions on paper.

I strongly encourage you to use a system of tracking your income and expenses that's easy for you to use and under-stand. If transactions aren't entered into a software program correctly, your software program is going to generate incor-rect profit and loss statements and other reports. I work with many clients who use accounting software that they don't fully understand. When it comes time to review their profit and loss statement for the year, they're not confident they recorded the transactions into the software correctly. Often times, they're forced to spend valuable time and money on identifying and correcting errors.

Income Recordkeeping

The easiest way to track all of the money you receive for selling a product or providing a service is to put it directly into your bank account. When it comes time to calculate your sales for the year, you can look at your bank statements to see all of the deposits you made from your sales. I strongly encourage you to do it this way because, if you're ever audited, the IRS is going to look at your bank statements and compare your deposits to the sales reported on your business tax return. Tracking and reporting your sales in this way will help ensure that the tax return matches your bank statements.

Expense Recordkeeping

There are three things you need in order to substantiate an expense on your tax return: (1) a ledger, (2) proof of the expense, and (3) proof that you paid for the expense.

A ledger is a list of all the expenses for the year for one type of expense. Below is an example of an advertising ledger.

Sample Advertising Ledger

Your Company Name For Period Ending December 31, 20XX		
Advertising Ledger		
DATE PAID	**DESCRIPTION**	**AMOUNT**
1/15/20XX	Magazine ad	$200.00
2/4/20XX	Newspaper ad	$350.00
3/22/20XX	Internet ad	$1,500.00
4/3/20XX	Coupon ad	$500.00
5/4/20XX	Magazine ad	$300.00
6/13/20XX	Newspaper ad	$450.00
7/25/20XX	Internet ad	$1,600.00
8/9/20XX	Coupon ad	$600.00
9/23/20XX	Magazine ad	$400.00
10/20/20XX	Newspaper ad	$550.00
11/5/20XX	Internet ad	$1,500.00
12/5/20XX	Coupon ad	$1,000.00
	Total	$8,950.00

Keep a ledger for each type of expense you have for your business. At the end of the year, combine the totals of each expense from the ledgers and subtract them from your sales to determine your profit or loss. This is called a Profit and Loss Statement or Income Statement. See the following example.

Sample Profit and Loss Statement

Your Company Name For Period Ending December 31, 20XX Cash Basis	
SALES	**Year to Date Amount**
Gross Sales	$1,000,000
Less Sales Returns and Allowances	$0
Net Sales	$1,000,000
COST OF SALES	
Cost of Goods Sold	$0
Gross Profit or (Loss)	$1,000,000
EXPENSES	
Salaries and Wages	$620,000
Vehicle	$23,465
Rent	$88,000
Taxes and Licenses	$1,346
Depreciation & Amortization	$6,507
Retirement Plans, etc.	$96,000
Advertising	$8,950
Entertainment (50%)	$4,067
Insurance	$10,156
Meals (50%)	$6,808
Supplies	$29,795
Travel	$13,677
Utilities	$5,647
Total Expenses	$914,418
NET INCOME/PROFIT OR (LOSS)	**$85,582**

Second, you need to have proof of your expense. This includes any documentation, such as an invoice, receipt, or lease agreement, that states the date of the transaction, what the expense was for, and the company or person you incurred the expense from.

Third, you need proof that you paid for the expense. This includes a bank statement, credit card statement, cashier's check, money order, or check. It also includes cash payments. I strongly recommend you do not pay expenses in cash because it makes it more difficult  to prove that you paid the expense and that you used cash that was already reported in sales as income.

Some expenses, such as meals, entertainment, and travel have additional recordkeeping requirements. Please review those respective sections previously discussed to ensure you have an understanding of how to record those expenses.

How do I substantiate my expenses?

1. Ledger

2. Proof of expense

3. Proof I paid for the expense

Estimated Taxes

As a business owner, you're not having taxes withheld as you would as an employee. Therefore, you have to make estimated tax payments. Estimated taxes are made quarterly. The due dates are typically April 15, June 15, September 15, and the following January 15 for the current year taxes owed. The purpose of paying estimated taxes on time, on a quarterly basis, is to avoid any penalties for paying your taxes late.

The calculation to determine your estimated taxes each quarter is complex. I highly recommend you talk to a tax professional to help you determine the correct amount of estimated taxes to make each quarter.

Estimated Tax Payments	Due Dates
Payment 1	April 15
Payment 2	June 15
Payment 3	September 15
Payment 4	January 15

Statute of Limitations

The tax laws limit the period in which the IRS may assess additional tax on you or audit you. This deadline is known as the statute of limitations. The statute of limitations is three years for federal tax purposes and is applicable to individual income tax returns (Form 1040) with or without a Schedule C (sole proprietorship) attached, partnership tax returns, and corporation tax returns.

The tax laws also give taxpayers three years to amend a federal tax return. The state tax laws where you live will determine the statute of limitations for your state income taxes. In California, it's four years rather than three years.

The statute of limitations is based on the filing date of your tax return. Individual income tax returns, such as a Form 1040 with or without a Schedule C, are due April 15. If a tax return is filed on or before this date, the statute of limitations begins on the due date, April 15. For example, if you file your 2013 individual income tax return on February 4, 2014 when it's due April 15, 2014, your return is considered as filed on April 15, 2014. Therefore, the IRS has until April 15, 2017 to audit your tax return and you have until April 15, 2017 to amend your tax return.

100 • Outsmarting the System

Chapter Summary

The methods learned throughout this chapter are valuable to new and existing business owners alike. Accurately tracking and reporting your business income and expenses will ensure you're on the right track for tax purposes. You can use the cash basis or accrual basis method of accounting to report your income and expenses. Most business owners, especially service providers, will use the cash basis method.

Be sure to report all of your income. You can write off any expenses that are ordinary and necessary. Think of your expenses as either 100% deductible or partially deductible. The most common partially deductible expenses are: (1) home office, (2) vehicle, (3) meals and entertainment, (4) travel, (5) depreciable assets, (6) cell phone, and (7) gifts.

You're required by law to maintain books and records that clearly reflect your income. For keeping track of your income, it's best to deposit all of the business income you receive into your bank account. For expenses, you need three things to support your deductions: (1) a ledger, (2) proof of the expense, and (3) proof that you paid the expense.

Since you don't have taxes taken out as a business owner as you would as an employee, you're required to make quarterly estimated tax payments. They're typically due April 15, June 15, September 15, and the following January 15 for the current year taxes owed. Lastly, remember the IRS has three years from the date your tax return was filed to audit you and assess additional tax. You also have three years to amend your tax return, if needed.

In the next chapter, we'll discuss trusted advisors and what the rich know that you don't about the IRS.

- CHAPTER 8 -

What the Rich Know that You Don't

Do you feel as though the rich have inside knowledge when it comes to the IRS? You're right! I worked at the IRS for over eight years and witnessed it first-hand. I was fortunate enough to be highly skilled at auditing tax returns; I typically found adjustments on each tax return I audited and closed a lot of audit cases. As a result, I was promoted quickly at the IRS. This provided me the opportunity to audit a wide range of businesses. I examined hundreds of businesses of all sizes, ranging from home based businesses, to businesses with multiple locations in the region, to multinational corporations. I also examined all of the owners and individuals related to these companies.

My unique insight into the IRS has provided me with information that's not known by some of the most experienced tax experts. If you're currently working with advisors in the tax or accounting industry, it may be beneficial to share with them the information in this chapter.

Trusted Advisors

A common trend among the rich is they're guided by the best and brightest professionals in the industry. They understand that a team of trusted advisors can provide them with complex strategies to outsmart the system. Through guidance from their trusted advisors, the rich strategically and confidently utilize the tax laws to their advantage. Armed with your own team of advisors and the strategies taught throughout this book, you'll be able to take advantage of tax laws in the same way as the rich.

It doesn't matter how smart you are, you can't be good at everything. Therefore, it's best to have a team of professionals to guide you in lowering your taxes by becoming an investor, landlord, and/or small business owner.

Here's a partial list of professionals you could hire to help you throughout your journey.

Professionals

Investments	Real Estate
Chartered Financial Analyst (CFA)	Commercial Broker
Certified Financial Planner (CFP)	Home Inspector
Financial Advisor	Real Estate Agent
Personal Financial Specialist (PFS)	Real Estate Appraiser
Tax	**Attorney**
Certified Public Accountant (CPA)	Business Attorney
Enrolled Agent (EA)	Estate Attorney
Tax Attorney	Real Estate Attorney

Other
Bookkeeper
Business Broker
Insurance Salesperson
Payroll Specialist

There are certain trusted advisors you should have on your team from the very beginning. You can add to your team as your needs change. If you want to become an investor, at the very least, you should have a financial advisor and a tax professional on your team. If you want to be a landlord, you should have a real estate attorney, a real estate agent, and a tax professional on your team. If you want to be a small business owner, you should have a business attorney and a tax professional on your team.

There are different ways to find trusted advisors. Talk to your friends and family and ask if they have anyone to refer you to. Consider asking one of your current trusted advisors, such as your tax preparer or attorney, for a referral. Word-of-mouth is the best way to find good advisors. Another option is to find online reviews of professionals. Some reviews may be unreliable, such as if the professional paid for the reviews. However, you can usually identify the legitimacy of the review based on the tone and details provided in the review.

I recommend you find a professional who (1) has experience with your issue, (2) you like to work with, and (3) you trust his or her judgment. You'll most likely be spending a lot of time with your trusted advisor, so it's important you enjoy being with him or her. Also, you want to feel comfortable asking questions and seeking guidance.

Do your homework and read up on what you're trying to achieve before you meet with a potential trusted advisor. Ask questions to test his or her level of expertise and views on pertinent issues. Use the answers to determine if he or she can properly guide you. Questioning the advisor will also help you determine if you enjoy working with him or her.

Not every question can be answered with a black and white answer. Consequently, the advice you receive may be ambiguous. Therefore, find a professional whose judgment you trust. You'll be able to get the most out of your relationship with your advisor when you're comfortable following his or her guidance.

The best example I can give you of a trusted advisor already in your life is your medical doctor, optometrist, or dentist. You go to these people because you like them and/or you trust their judgment.

IRS

Through their advisors, the rich have an in-depth understanding of the government agencies that regulate small businesses. Small businesses are regulated by many government agencies, such as the IRS, Department of Labor, Secretary of State, state taxing agency for state income tax, payroll tax, sales tax, and any local or city agencies. Out of all the agencies you need to worry about, the IRS is the most important. The IRS has the most resources available to perform tax audits. In addition, the IRS reviews your tax information every year, whereas other government agencies are in contact less frequently.

Many states don't have the resources necessary to conduct audits as thoroughly as the IRS does. When the IRS has an adjustment at the federal level, there's typically a similar adjustment at the state level. For income and payroll taxes, the state taxing agencies piggyback off of the IRS audits. They're able to receive money through the audits without having to commit their own limited resources to conduct an audit.

Many state tax agencies are more concerned with taxpayers paying their taxes and filing the correct tax forms. The IRS is also concerned with this, but they have the resources to do a more thorough examination to ensure a taxpayer is in compliance with the complex tax laws and to find fraud.

IRS Operating Divisions

The IRS has four operating divisions: Wage and Investment (W&I), Tax Exempt and Government Entities (TEGE), Small Business/Self-Employed (SBSE), and Large Business and International (LB&I). In regards to audits, each of these divisions has a different focus in ensuring a taxpayer's compliance with the complex U.S. tax laws.

The W&I division primarily focusses on examining individuals (non-business owners). The TEGE division focusses on examining employee plans, such as a 401(k) or a SEP-IRA, exempt organizations, such as a charitable organization or a religious organization, and government entities.

The SBSE division primarily focusses on examining businesses with less than $10 million in assets. This is approximately 50 million taxpayers. The LB&I division focusses on examining businesses with $10 million or more in assets. This is approximately 100,000 taxpayers. I started my career working in the SBSE division and was promoted quickly to the LB&I division.

Audit Rate

The rich are aware of the time limit for audits and audit risk. The rich know that the IRS typically has three years to audit them. We discussed this statute of limitations in Chapter 7.

Since the rich recognize that the IRS is the most important agency to be worried about, they examine the IRS's audit rates and approximate their own chances of being audited. The rich understand that the audit rate for being a business owner is very slim overall. The rich know that, of the different types of business owners, sole proprietors have the highest audit rate. They also know that the risk of being audited is lower for business owners who choose to file as an S corporation or partnership.

You can see the audit rates by looking at the IRS Data Book on the IRS's website. According to the IRS 2012 Data Book, during fiscal year 2012 (October 1, 2011 through September 30, 2012), the IRS processed more than 237.3 million federal tax returns and supplemental documents. Over 146.2 million of these were individual income tax returns filed, which accounted for over 61.6% of all returns filed.

Individual tax returns audited that had business income filing as a sole proprietorship had a 1.2% to 3.7% examination rate in fiscal year 2012. As the company's sales increased, so did the audit rate. Partnership and S Corporation tax returns had a 0.5% examination rate. Small C Corporations had an examination rate that varied between 0.7% to 2.6%. As the size of the assets increased, the audit rate increased as well. Small C Corporations are defined as having less than $10 million in assets and are not filing as a cooperative association or a foreign corporation.

Examination Rates in Fiscal Year 2012

Type of Return	Examination Rate
Sole Proprietorship	1.2% - 3.7%
Partnership	0.50%
S Corporation	0.50%
Small C Corporation*	0.7% - 2.6%

*Small C Corporations are defined as having less than $10 million in assets and are not filing as a cooperative association or a foreign corporation.

The rich also know that the odds are slim that, if audited, the IRS auditor will be truly motivated to find all of the errors. This lack of motivation among IRS auditors is because there is no incentive for the auditor to find a lot of adjustments. Within a for-profit organization, it's common for the employees to be motivated to do a good job due to incentives such as money, promotions, or time off. The IRS doesn't reward its employees in this manner for finding a lot of tax adjustments. The IRS encourages its employees to close as many audit cases as possible in a fiscal year, regardless if there were any adjustments or not. Furthermore, the IRS rewards its employees for closing audit cases by noting their productivity in their yearly evaluation. How's that for government efficiency!

As a result, the rich also understand that a very high percentage of tax returns examined result in no changes. A no change means that the auditor concluded there were no material adjustments to be made that would result in a recommendation for additional tax to be paid.

Types of IRS Audits

The IRS has three types of audits: (1) correspondence, (2) office, and (3) field. A correspondence audit is conducted through the mail. An office audit is conducted at your local IRS office with an auditor face-to-face. A field audit is conducted at your place of business with an auditor face-to-face. The IRS 2012 Data Book shows the percentage of returns audited that resulted in a no-change for (1) a field audit (including an office audit) and (2) a correspondence audit.

The IRS 2012 Data Book stated that the individual tax returns audited in fiscal year 2012 that had business income filing as a sole proprietorship had a 6.0% to 13.0% chance of a field audit being a no change and an 8.0% to 50.0% chance of a correspondence audit being a no change. Partnership tax returns had a 44.0% chance of a field audit being a no change and a 38.0% chance of a correspondence audit being a no change. S Corporation tax returns had a 33.0% chance of a field audit being a no change and a 44.0% chance of a correspondence audit being a no change. Small C Corporation tax returns had a 16.0% to 35.0% chance of a field audit being a no change and a 39.0% to 66.0% chance of a correspondence audit being a no change. These are some high no change rates!

Examination No-Change Rates in Fiscal Year 2012

Type of Return	Field Audit	Correspondence Audit
Sole Proprietorship	6.0% - 13.0%	8.0% - 50.0%
Partnership	44.0%	38.0%
S Corporation	33.0%	44.0%
Small C Corporation*	16.0% - 35.0%	39.0% - 66.0%

*Small C Corporations are defined as having less than $10 million in assets and are not filing as a cooperative association or a foreign corporation.

IRS Audit Procedures

The rich know that if you do get a motivated auditor, the IRS procedures put so much pressure on the auditor to close cases rather than discover material adjustments that many incorrect tax positions could be missed. A tax position is interpreting the complex tax laws and applying them to your facts and circumstances. For instance, the determination that a sale be reported in this year, and not the following year, is a tax position.

As I mentioned earlier, the IRS auditors are encouraged and motivated to close as many audits or cases in the shortest time possible. This is typically 3 to 6 months in the SBSE division or 9 to 12 months in the LB&I division for a field audit. These time frames might appear to be long to you, but they're not when compared to the burdensome procedures the auditor must follow and the number of audits he or she is conducting at the time. It'll take the auditor a long time to open a new audit, follow the correct procedures, and close the case off in full compliance with the IRS review process.

In other words, the rich know that the IRS trains its auditors to focus more on procedures and close cases quickly rather than trying to find every possible adjustment on a tax return.

Reasonable Basis

Let's say the auditor does find some material adjustments that could lead to more tax. The rich know that the tax laws and IRS procedures are written in their favor so long as they're cooperative during the audit and didn't do anything fraudulent. The rich know that all they need to have is a reasonable basis for their position and the odds of it being partially or completely upheld are good.

Three Levels to Have Case Heard

The rich know that there are three levels to have their case heard if they're subject to an audit: (1) examination, (2) appeals, and (3) tax court. During the examination process, the auditor's goal is to examine a taxpayer's tax return to ensure it's in compliance with the U.S. tax laws. The burden of proof is on the taxpayer to prove any tax positions and to substantiate any amounts on the return. The burden of proof switches to the government when there's an increase to income or fraud. Therefore, the rich know to always report their income, don't do anything fraudulent, and use the tax laws to their favor so long as they have a reasonable basis for their tax positions.

Three Levels to Have Tax Case Heard

3. Tax Court	**Final Chance**
2. Appeals	⇧
1. Starts in Examination	⇧

If the auditor cannot be persuaded that a tax position is in compliance with the U.S. tax laws at the examination level, the rich don't care. They aren't concerned because they know that the auditor's job is to hold them to the letter of the law and if it's gray, the auditor will err on the side of caution and make an adjustment. As a result, the rich know to have their case sent to the Office of Appeals.

The appeal officer's job is to keep the case out of court and settle. Why? Because if the case goes to court and the taxpayer wins, it'll set precedence for the whole nation and become primary authority for other taxpayers to use based on similar facts and circumstances. This is called the hazards of litigation. The rich know that examination's job is a lot different than appeals' job. Appeals has the right to negotiate and settle a case whereas examination doesn't.

For instance, let's say you wrote off travel expenses and the auditor didn't agree that these expenses were ordinary and necessary and the adjustment resulted in a recommendation that an additional $10,000 in taxes be paid. If you have a reasonable basis or argument for why these travel expenses are deductible, understand that the auditor's job is to look at the tax laws as black and white. If the laws are unclear, the auditor will err on the side of caution and make an adjustment. You need to be confident in your tax position and request the case be sent to appeals. In appeals, their job is to settle the case, if possible, by looking at the facts and circumstances, the tax laws, and the hazards of litigation to come to an agreement with you.

Let's say the appeals officer gives you an offer to settle the case for $6,000. You're going to take this offer for three reasons. First, you'll owe the $6,000 for this year, but you may have gotten away with a similar tax position in previous years and the IRS only caught you for this year. It's similar to speeding on the freeway every single day and after years of not getting caught, you finally get a speeding ticket.

Second, you'll have to pay interest on the $6,000, but the current interest rate is approximately 3%, which is lower than any credit card rate, mortgage interest loan or bank loan that you can receive today. If you file as a C Corporation, you have the added bonus of being able to deduct the interest paid.

Third, as long as you have a reasonable basis for your tax position and weren't negligent, you can most likely get out of any accuracy related penalties, which are 20%.

Chapter Summary

The rich understand that to be wealthy in America, it's best to be self-employed. The rich are guided by the best and brightest in the industry. With their guidance, the rich strategically take advantage of the tax laws that favor small business owners.

They realize the importance of the IRS. They also realize that as long as they have a reasonable basis for any tax positions they take, they report all of their income, and don't do anything fraudulent, the odds of the tax position being partially or completely upheld are really good.

The rich know that there are three levels to have their case heard: (1) examination, (2) appeals, and (3) tax court. If examination doesn't agree with their position, the wealthy will take their case to the Office of Appeals. Appeals will more likely than not settle the case due to the hazards of litigation. The wealthy don't have a problem paying the additional tax owed because they may have gotten away with this tax position in previous years, the interest rate is roughly 3% on the tax owed, and they can get out of penalties by proving that they had a reasonable basis for their position.

The U.S. tax laws and IRS procedures are written the same for you and the rich. You can take advantage of these strategies in the same way as the rich. Consult with your tax advisor and/or read IRS publications and other tax related materials to learn more.

- CHAPTER 9 -

Next Steps

In order to get the most out of this book, there is one requirement: start applying what you've read. As poet Ralph Waldo Emerson said, "An ounce of action is worth a ton of theory." To help you develop a solid basis for your plan of action, let's review what we've discussed.

Go back to the Contents page of this book. Review this page as a reminder of the concepts we discussed throughout the book. Next, flip through each page, reading only the headings and subheadings until you get to this chapter.

In as few words as possible, write down the major points you learned from this book. You can write it below or on a separate piece of paper. Please do this before proceeding to the next section.

....

....

....

....

....

....

Outsmarting the System

What Did I Learn?

Your list may include the following concepts and strategies:

- ✧ My goal is to reach financial freedom.

- ✧ The system misleads people. However, the rich know how to outsmart the system.

- ✧ Taxes are my largest expense; they prevent me from reaching financial freedom faster.

- ✧ If I want to lower my taxes, I need to change the way I make money.

- ✧ Becoming an investor, landlord, and/or small business owner will enable me to take advantage of the tax laws and reach financial freedom faster.

- ✧ Becoming a small business owner is the best path to pursue because the tax benefits are the greatest and the costs to start a venture are low.

- ✧ I should start a service business.

- ✧ My goal for my business is to make as much profit as possible.

- ✧ By following these steps, I will outsmart the system.

I highly recommend that all taxpayers, including you, should be a small business owner. Therefore, let's review your next steps for becoming a business owner. If you already own a business, use these as a guideline to ensure your business stays on track. If you're passionate about becoming an investor or landlord, I recommend you do research before taking any action and talk to professionals to help you.

Business Idea

You can sell a product or provide a service. At the very least, you need to come up with a service business idea. Decide what product or service you can provide to start your own business.

Write down a few ideas of a product or service you would like to provide. Refer to the list in Chapter 6 for examples.

....

....

....

....

....

....

....

....

....

....

....

....

....

....

....

Purpose and Differentiation

Your business must have a purpose. That purpose should be one of two things: (1) fill a need or (2) solve a problem. It is essential to differentiate your business from competitors. Your differentiation should align with your business purpose.

Write down your business idea, business purpose, and how you're going to differentiate your business from your competition.

....

....

....

....

....

....

....

....

....

....

....

....

....

....

Sales Skills

If you don't know how to sell, you need to learn now. The easiest ways to learn how to sell are to read books and talk to friends or family who do sales. You can search for books on the Internet and either purchase them or get them at your local library. I encourage you to keep your costs to a minimum, so borrow books from a library for free.

Once you understand how to sell, you can start applying what you learned. Not everyone sells the same. You need to find your own style that works for you. The beauty of sales versus any other skill is that it's very measurable and clear-cut: you either made the sale or you didn't. Your goal is to hone in your sales skill so you can make a lot of money.

Write down your strengths and weaknesses in regards to your ability to sell. How will you learn or improve your sales skills?

....

....

....

....

....

....

....

....

....

Educate Yourself

Continue to educate yourself. Utilize classes, books, and on-line articles to learn more. Read as much as you can. Talk to similar professionals or find a mentor to guide you. No one path or training is going to guarantee your venture will be a success. Find what works for you.

What are you going to learn about first? Write it down.

....

....

....

....

....

....

....

....

....

....

....

....

....

....

....

Trusted Advisors

It's often more advantageous to be proactive in searching for trusted advisors. If you start searching early, you'll have more time to research them thoroughly. If you're forced to hurry and find a trusted advisor in response to an emergency situation, you won't have adequate time to ensure he or she is the right fit for you. I strongly encourage you to think about which advisors you'll need in the future and find them now. When you need them, you'll already have them on your team.

Identify the types of professionals that you'll need on your team. Write them down.

....

....

....

....

....

....

....

....

....

....

....

....

Too often people rush through a book, get a few good ideas, put the book aside, and forget about the ideas. This exercise was designed to help you remember what you read and identify your next steps. Keep your notes and refer to them, and this book, often. Re-reading this information will help you keep the points clearly in mind. You may wish to review this book on a monthly basis as a source of motivation. Regard this as a starting point to reach financial freedom. Whenever you're feeling beat by the system, implement the steps learned here.

Final Words

The system has programmed you to believe the path to success is to go to school, get good grades, get a job, get a promotion, make more money, buy a house, and put money into a retirement account. This system has fooled you. As you make more money as an employee, you pay more taxes.

As your largest expense, taxes can prevent you from reaching financial freedom. Financial freedom is having enough money saved to support your lifestyle without working. The sooner you reach financial freedom, the better. The only way to decrease your taxes is to change the way you make money. You can do this by becoming an investor, landlord, and/or a small business owner.

With the new knowledge you have learned from this book, you'll be able to lower your taxes, control your future, and reach financial freedom. The change isn't going to happen overnight, but with a plan, you can put this new knowledge into action. You'll be able to join the rich in outsmarting the system.

Remember, only you can make the change for yourself. This book is meant to enlighten you and get the process started for you, but now it's up to you to come up with a plan and take action. It can be done. Your ability to overcome challenges you face during your journey will guarantee you success. Life presents challenges to those who can handle them. Good luck on your journey!

Made in the USA
Charleston, SC
14 January 2014